INTIMATE LIFE MINISTRIES

Experiencing God in Marriage, Family and the Church

A Handbook For Reclaiming
Marriage and Family as Divine Relationships

Intimacy Press

Intimacy Press

P.O. Box 201808, Austin, Texas, 78720-1808

(800) 881-8008   (512) 795-0498   Fax (512) 795-0853

U.K. 080+096-6685

ISBN-0-9642845-5-3

Intimate Life Ministries

Contents

Chapter 6 - Additional Material on the Intimate Life Message

Chapter 7 - Intimacy Research Findings
Chapter 8 - Intimate Life Resources

Dedication

"The land is still ours because we have sought the Lord our God; we sought Him and He has given us rest" (II Chronicles 14:7).

Marriages and families are HIS land!

This resource is offered with special dedication to . . .

◆ The **Lord,** who *"is intimate with the upright"* (Proverbs 3:32 NAS).

◆ The **Intimate Life** network of churches and other ministries who are co-laboring to establish comprehensive, ongoing ministries which deepen our intimacy with God, in marriage, family and the church. While using **Intimate Life** publications and other resources, homes, churches and communities are being "fortified" against such enemies as divorce, abuse and neglect — providing places of refuge, security and rest.

◆ The **Intimate Life** ministry associates — a network of pastors, ministers and other Christian leaders who seek to walk intimately with God and with others in their marriages, families and churches. As these associates faithfully teach the Word, they benefit from specific **Intimate Life** principles and then are able to impart these principles to others.

For further information on how you might be a part of making an impact on marriages and families in your church or community, contact:

Experiencing God in Marriage, Family and the Church

Intimate Life Ministries
P.O. Box 201808
Austin, Texas 78720-1808

Telephone: U.S. 800+881-8008
or 512+795-0498
FAX 512+795-0853
U.K. 080+096-6685

◆ *Center for Marriage and Family Intimacy* ◆ *Intimacy Press*
◆ *Galatians 6:6 Ministry* ◆ *Intimate Life Communications*
◆ *Intimacy Institute* ◆ *Worship Connection*

Intimate Life Ministries

Experiencing God in Marriage, Family and the Church

The primary goal of Intimate Life Ministries is to help establish ongoing marriage and family ministries and ministries which encourage intimacy with God - within the church. Currently, more than 3000 churches across America and in several foreign countries are using Intimate Life materials, resources, and training seminars to establish a comprehensive ministry that addresses all aspects of marriage and family relationships (marriage, parenting, preparing for marriage, being single, divorce recovery, and restoring relationships) and intimacy with God (both individually and corporately).

Many churches have adopted the name *Intimate Life* as the name of this ministry. Subtitled "Experiencing God in Marriage, Family and the Church," the name communicates many of the basic biblical truths which are vital to developing and maintaining meaningful relationships with God and others.

Intimate - God created us with a need to relate intimately both with Himself and others. Shallow relationships will not satisfy our deep longings for emotional and spiritual connection with God and others. Intimate relationships, built upon affectionate caring, vulnerable communication, joint accomplishment, and mutual giving and support *will* fulfill this longing of the human soul.

Life - The abundant life which Christ promised in John 10:10 is not dependent upon position, possession, or circumstances. We experience abundant living through meaningful relationships with God, family and friends. The apostle Paul emphasized the importance of sharing one's life with meaningful others when he said, *"We loved you so much that we were delighted to share with you not only the gospel of God but our lives as well, because you had become so dear to us"* (1 Thessalonians 2:8).

Experiencing God . . .
Because *"Every good and perfect gift is from above, coming down from the Father of the heavenly lights"* (James 1:17), we must appropriate the flow of God's life and provision if we are to relate intimately with others. We must receive: *His* comfort before we can comfort others (2 Corinthians 1:3-4), *His* forgiveness before we can forgive (Ephesians 4:32), *His* acceptance before we can accept others (Romans 15:7), and *His* love if we're to love one another (John 15: 12). The spiritual principle of Matthew 10:8, *"Freely you received, freely give"* dictates that we must first *receive* God's divine "commodities"— His "manifold" grace, before we can give them to others (I Peter 4:10).

... In Marriage, Family and the Church

In addition to our intimate walk with God, He has divinely ordained three human relationships through which our need for intimacy can be fulfilled on a horizontal level: marriage (Genesis 2), the family (Genesis 4, Psalm 127:3), and the church (Matthew 16).

The deeply felt, God-given intimacy needs that we all have can be abundantly satisfied as we lovingly and deliberately receive and give God's divine grace through His ordained relationships.

CHAPTER ONE
Intimate Life Ministries

Our Purpose
The Mission of Intimate Life Ministries

What is the Intimate Life Ministry? We are . . .

- ◆ A network of **Churches** seeking to fortify homes in their churches and communities.

- ◆ A network of **Pastors and other ministry leaders,** walking intimately with God and their families and seeking to live vulnerably before their people.

- ◆ A team of **Regional Coordinator couples** in key cities committed to helping churches establish ongoing marriage and family ministries.

- ◆ A team of **Professional Associates** from ministry and other professional Christian backgrounds, assisting with research, training, and resource development.

- ◆ **Christian broadcasters,** media, and other affiliates cooperating to see marriages and families reclaimed as divine relationships.

- ◆ **Headquarters staff** providing strategic planning, coordination, and support.

What is the Intimate Life Ministry's mission?

> *To assist individuals, churches and other ministries in the development of Intimate Life ministries — ongoing ministries which deepen our intimacy with God and with each other in marriage, family and the Church.*

First, our mission is to assist in the *establishment of "ministries," rather than programs.* A ministry will include various programs, but a ministry is more than programs. Ministries are considered essential to the overall health and vitality of the church. People don't attend a ministry just once or twice—they continually participate, regularly experiencing the key dimensions and blessings of a ministry. In most churches, the worship service with its various components would be an example of an essential ministry. Other essential ministries might include education, nursery, youth, or evangelism. Our goal is to establish marriage and family ministries which are valued just as highly as other church ministries—and which enjoy a similar level of commitment, priority, and involvement.

Second, to be truly effective, these *ministries must have* ongoing *opportunities for people to be involved*, rather than just occasional emphases. In many churches, the marriage and family "ministry" consists of a once a year sermon or sermon series and maybe a 6 – 12 week class. Perhaps a pastor also offers counseling to troubled couples. Certainly these types of help are better than nothing at all, but they hardly represent an ongoing ministry. An ongoing ministry provides a variety of both preventative and corrective help for marriages and families. And this help is **regularly** available to most if not all the members of the congregation and their immediate community, just as the worship ministry is regularly available.

Third, we are working to help pastors and committed lay leaders to *establish these ongoing ministries in the* **local church,** rather than in counseling centers or other organizations. We believe that the church, the "family of God," is God's chosen vehicle to accomplish the work He has ordained (Matthew 16:18). The agendas of many churches are crowded with other causes, and church pastors and leaders have numerous demands upon their time and energy. But if the church doesn't respond to the current marriage and family crisis with meaningful, practical, low-cost, readily available help, most people will not be able to find that help anywhere else. (See "Should Your Church Have a Marriage and Family Ministry?" on page 38, for further detail regarding the crucial role of the church.)

Fourth, we believe that **intimacy** is the quality in relationships which we all long for and for which we were created. Thus, *ongoing ministries in local churches would seek to promote intimacy in all relationship*s. What do we mean by intimacy? "Intimacy" in the Old Testament speaks of a deep mutual "knowing" of another person as both become caringly involved in each other's lives (Job 19:14; Psalm 139:3; Proverbs 3:32). Marriage intimacy is the mutual freedom to share all of one's self—body, soul, and spirit—with your spouse. Our enemy is not only sin, but also isolation from others. We would do better in our struggles against sin if we were meaningfully involved in intimate relationships, openly sharing our very lives with others (I Thessalonians 2:8-9).

Finally, *the most important Person for us to have an intimate relationship with is God Himself.* Therefore, an effective ongoing marriage and family ministry in a local church will help husbands, wives, single adults, youth and children deepen their intimacy **with God** (Philippians 3:10).

Why Is This Mission So Important?

We are engaged in a war for the family.

Some have called it a "culture war." Dr. James Dobson calls it a "great civil war of values." This war is being fought in the U.S., the United Kingdom, throughout Europe and literally around the world. Because the U. S. is the world leader in divorce, over 70% of American children will spend some of their growing up years in a single parent home. Children from these homes are three times more likely to drop out of school than children from intact families. They are four times more likely to develop drug problems and/or to commit a crime. We are all familiar with the staggering increase in cases of child abuse and neglect. What often goes unreported is the sad fact that a child from a broken home is many times more likely to be abused or neglected than a child from an intact home—the abuse often coming through step-relationships or a live-in boy/girl friend.

Even if we did not have such heart-numbing statistics, who has not been touched personally by the tragedy of divorce? Who has not been affected in some manner by the high rate of miserable or empty marriages? One predictable spillover of all this is reported by many who are involved in ministry with single adults—the increasingly large number of "never-marrieds" who are afraid to marry at all. These adults, in their 30's and even 40's are themselves often products of broken homes. Many would rather risk a lifetime of being alone than possibly experience again the trauma of a family being torn apart.

Whether or not we can demonstrate the damage statistically and culturally, we know that God Himself is the Creator of marriage and the family. We know with absolute certainty that He desires not merely for families to stay together, but for every family member to have great joy and satisfaction from the intimacy of their family experience. We can be equally certain that the enemy is doing everything in his power to "kill, steal, and destroy" first the intimacy, and then the intactness of every marriage and family.

Traditional church programs which sought to meet the needs of marriage and families are becoming inadequate. What did the church do in the past when someone was struggling with family difficulties? We suspect that mature couples got involved—that informal "mentoring" of the less mature was conducted by couples and families who "came alongside" to model, instruct, and admonish if necessary. Perhaps the Titus 2 model of pastors teaching the older men to be "temperate, worthy of respect, self-controlled, and sound in faith, in love, and in endurance" was more widely practiced. This passage also directs pastors to teach the older women certain important character qualities so that these women can then teach the younger women to be good wives and mothers. How many of our churches have significant numbers of men and women who can mentor the large numbers of younger couples who need and often want guidance, support, and solid examples of satisfying marital intimacy? A very transient society and the breakdown of extended families has added to this vacuum of needed role models and mentors.

The advent and expansion of "biblical" Christian counseling may have filled this void in many situations in the past. However, factors such as affordability and availability of truly biblical counseling are bringing many hurting people back to the church seeking help. Is it reasonable to expect pastors to handle this heavy load? Many provide marriage and family counseling, but most admit that crises among their members determine their counseling hours, rather than divine calling. Help for marriages and families must come from the church, but we cannot expect the pastoral staff to be solely responsible. Rather than a model of people being helped by degreed "experts," Intimate Life Ministries are built around the saints being equipped for the work of the ministry—equipped to encourage others to meet with God at the point of His Word.

Marriages and families can be helped, and they **are** *being helped!*

Currently more than 3000 churches across America, the United Kingdom, other parts of Europe and elsewhere are using the Intimate Life materials, resources, and leadership development conferences to comprehensively address all aspects of personal relationships: marriage, parenting, divorce recovery, and single adults. Thousands of people are learning how to experience genuine intimacy in all relationships:

A minister's wife from England writes, "This dimension of 'leaving father and mother' has never been fully explained before. As I venture into sharing with my spouse the hurts/joys of my childhood, I anticipate his compassion and care so that we can mourn together about losses in our early life."

Missionaries from Hungary write, "My wife and I have been on the mission field for twelve years—the past six without our children. Our problems with the 'empty nest' syndrome have made this difficult. The Galatians 6:6 seminar has given new insights and renewed hope in how we can work through this area more effectively."

"We found freedom from the bondage of past hurts and have become more intimate in a deeper way than I have ever experienced before." – a couple in Arizona.

"We have experienced a healing and restoration which we will share with other couples as we implement a Marriage and Family ministry in our urban church. In our inner city ministry we know that many of the problems faced by these residents can be circumvented by this type of ministry." – a couple in Louisiana, USA

"We were committed, but miserable. And our children were unhappy as well. We had no joy or satisfaction in our marriage. Intimate Life not only told us what we needed to do, but how to do it—how to heal hurts from the past, how to recognize and meet needs, and how to truly leave father and mother. Our marriage is now our chief source of happiness and abundance." – a couple from Oklahoma, USA

These and many others are being helped by Intimate Life leaders who often hold no advanced degrees in theology or counseling. These leaders are regular people who first wanted to deepen the intimacy in their own relationships. As they received benefit, they then began to help others experience the intimacy for which each of us longs.

Various Facets of Intimate Life Ministries

Intimate Life Ministries is a non-profit ministry whose purpose is to: Assist individuals, churches, and other ministries in the development of Intimate Life Ministries—ongoing ministries which deepen our intimacy with God and with others in marriage, family, and the church. Intimate Life Ministries is multi-faceted:

The Center for Marriage and Family Intimacy (CMFI) – provides instruction and materials to assist homes, churches and cities in becoming "fortified" against enemies such as divorce, abuse, and neglect—providing places of refuge, security, and rest.

Galatians 6:6 Ministry – provides special ministry to Christian leaders. Intimacy Retreats and other events, designed especially for ministry couples, are hosted in key cities throughout the United States and in other countries, offering times of restoration, renewal, and equipping. (See the detailed description of the Intimacy Retreats on following pages.)

Intimate Life Communications – provides radio, television, video, and audio support to Intimate Life Ministries and to participating churches. (See detailed description on following pages.)

Intimacy Institute – provides training for Christian professionals in various disciplines. Through the Institute, training in "Intimacy Therapy" is provided to professional and pastoral counselors. The Institute provides training and assistance to ministries and business leaders.

Intimacy Press – is the publishing/distributing arm of the ministry. It produces and distributes resources which uniquely address the intimacy message.

Worship Connection – assists individuals and churches in the area of intimacy with God. Through materials, conferences, and pastor/worship leader networks, it promotes the message of genuine worship—both individually and corporately. (See detailed description on following pages.)

Intimate Life Ministries is assisted by the ministry of Professional Associates and a network of pastors, ministry leaders and regional co-ordinators.

Galatians 6:6 Ministry

. . . ministering to Ministers

"Let those who are taught the Word share all good things with those who teach" (Galatians 6:6).

Fuller Institute of Church Growth — 1991 Survey of Pastors

◆ 80% believe that pastoral ministry is negatively affecting their families

◆ 70% do not have someone they would consider a close friend

◆ 37% have been involved in inappropriate sexual behavior with someone in the church

◆ 70% have a lower self-image after they've pastored than when they started

◆ 50% felt unable to meet the needs of the job

◆ 90% felt they were not adequately trained to cope in the ministry

◆ 40% reported a serious conflict with a church member at least once a month

---

An important part of the Intimate Life ministry is our burden for couples in the ministry. We are concerned that:

— Couples in the ministry often become so involved in "giving to others" that their personal lives are neglected. They inadvertently miss out on the first part of the spiritual equation found in Matthew 10:8, *"Freely you have received,* freely give." *The Galatians 6:6 Ministry provides Intimacy Retreats as a time of personal refreshment and renewal for those in the ministry.*

— A minister will not, on a regular basis, emphasize spiritual principles which are not real in his/her life. If a minister does not have a meaningful and fulfilling marriage and family, he/she will not aggressively support an ongoing ministry to marriages and families in the church. *A Galatians 6:6 Intimacy Retreat ministers to ministry couples in the area of their own marriage and family.*

Galatians 6:6 Intimacy Retreats are held in various cities across America and in other countries and are provided free of charge to ministry couples. The conference, hotel room, meals, and all materials are a gift from the ministry.

The typical schedule is:

First Day	9:00 a.m. – 9:15 a.m.	Registration: Conference Hotel
	9:15 a.m. – 12:00 p.m.	Intimacy Overview
		Lunch plus Hotel Room Check-in
	1:30 p.m. – 6:00 p.m.	Marriage Intimacy Workshop — Part I
	Evening	Dinner in the Restaurant or Room Service
		Couple Homework
Second Day	9:00 a.m. – 12:00 p.m.	Marriage Intimacy Workshop — Part II
		Lunch
	1:30 p.m. – 4:00 p.m.	Intimate Life Ministry in the Local Church
	4:00 p.m.	Dismiss

What others have said about the retreat:

An incredible get-away for my wife and me! My wife is the most important "earthly" priority I have...but I've never been able to express that in ways she could experience and feel. It happened this weekend! Thanks! – Pastor from Georgia, USA

You may never know the appreciation and love we have within us because of this ministry. You have given us hope and helped us to deal with hurts and experience true forgiveness. – Pastor from Texas, USA

As a husband, father and pastor, this weekend has opened up a new beginning to my marriage through the opportunity to be vulnerable and receive the Lord's comfort and healing through my wife. – Pastor from London, England

I feel that, finally, through this ministry, I have experienced a vital answer to the question "Who cares for the caregivers?" As the recipient of lavished grace, care and attention directed towards my wife and I, I am blessed and motivated to go on serving, caring and freely giving. – Pastor from Dublin, Ireland

For more information call: (in the U.S.) 1-800-881-8008
(in the U.K.) 080+096-6685

The Worship Connection

Intimacy with God is a prerequisite for intimacy with others. It's impossible to give something that you have not received. Since God is the source of "divine commodities" such as comfort, forgiveness, acceptance and love, we must constantly be receiving from Him if we are to give to others. Likewise, how we relate to meaningful others (spouse, family, friends) will affect our relationship with God. One of the basic tenets of Intimate Life Ministries is that we were created with a need to relate intimately both with God and meaningful others. We need to relate intimately to God through worship, communion and prayer and to others through marriage, family and the church.

The Worship Connection is a ministry sponsored by Intimate Life Ministries. It is a network of pastors and worship leaders who are:

◆ Learning to "walk together" in worship (Amos 3:3).

◆ Sharing their lives with one another (I Thessalonians 2:8).

◆ Sharing resources (Acts 4:32).

◆ Mentoring and discipling one another (Philippians 4:9).

◆ Removing the "alone-ness" of the ministry (Galatians 6:2).

◆ Learning more about worship (II Timothy 2:15).

◆ Unifying the body of Christ through worship (Revelation 7:9-10).

During the fall of 1994 and the spring of 1995, the concept of having a local Worship Connection Chapter has been field tested in the Dallas–Ft. Worth Metroplex. Worship leaders from 20-25 area churches began meeting once a month to pray together, worship, and study worship. A National Praise and Worship Conference was hosted by these churches in the summer of 1995, climaxing with a joint "God with Us" worship service involving several thousand people from more than 20 churches, from nearly a dozen different denominations.

The Worship Connection involves churches and individuals of all denominations. If you would be interested in starting a Worship Connection Chapter in your city, contact the Intimate Life Ministries office.

Intimate Life Communications

The Intimate Life Ministry provides radio and television resources and programming to the public and as support to network churches. Media products are now available to local broadcasters and churches in a variety of formats:

Radio Productions –

◆ *Intimate Life,* a daily half-hour radio program with host, Mike Frazier. Mike and the Intimate Life team of Professional Associates, Regional Coordinators and Pastoral Associates, challenge listeners to experience intimacy in important life relationships. Topics have recently included: Sex and Intimacy, Straight Thinking, Aloneness, Giving Worth to Kids, Leaving and Cleaving, The Intimate Life Message and Emotional Responding . . . each program giving listeners "homework" they can experience and apply. *Intimate Life* will be promoted and distributed nationally in the coming year. If your station is interested in airing *Intimate Life,* call Mike Frazier at 1-800-881-8008.

◆ *Intimate Moments,* a daily, one-minute radio program that provides practical "how-to's" and biblical insights into deepening important relationships. Available, free, to all requesting stations.

◆ Radio Specials – one-hour radio programs designed to explore, in depth, the applications of intimacy principles and issues such as the Healing Power of Intimacy and An Intimate Encounter; free to all stations.

Video Productions –

To assist local, cooperating churches, the Intimate Life ministry has available a wide variety of video tapes and "interactive" series:

◆ *Top 10 Intimacy Needs:* Created for "The Family Enrichment Series" on the ACTS and FamilyNet television systems, *The Top 10 Intimacy Needs* package utilizes the entire Intimate Life Team on a step-by-step journey through the material in the book authored by Dr. David Ferguson and Dr. Don McMinn. The video segments are suitable for individual, home or church group use, and includes both books and videos.

◆ *Intimate Encounters Workbook Series:* This recently completed video series with Dr. David and Teresa Ferguson is a comprehensive video supplement to the *Intimate Encounters Workbook.* Participants are given specific instructions and homework in a format that is perfect for home or church groups.

◆ Video Topics – Intimate Life Professional and Pastoral Associates speak on a variety of issues and topics, including these individual tapes and sets which were produced at the Pursuit of Intimacy National Conference, held in Austin, Texas, October 1994:

> *The Intimate Life Message* – David Ferguson
>
> *Parenting with Intimacy* – Paul Warren
>
> *Children as Gifts from the Lord* – Terri Ferguson
>
> *The Healing Power of Intimacy* – Robert Hemfelt
>
> *Perfectionism vs. Excellence* – Chris Thurman
>
> *Intimacy with God Video Set* – Don McMinn, Max Lucado, Peter Lord and Crawford Loritts
>
> *Parenting with Intimacy Video Set* – David Ferguson, Terri Ferguson, Paul Warren and Josh McDowell
>
> *Intimate Relationships Video Set* – Chris Thurman, Robert Hemfelt, Roger Barrier and Dennis Rainey
>
> . . . and many others, call for details.

Local Church Support –

In support of local church ministries, Intimate Life now provides radio production services, customized announcements and promotions for:

◆ Participating church Intimate Life ministries, classes, groups and counseling.

◆ Leadership Development Conferences in the area.

◆ Local church pastors, in promoting the *Intimate Life Sermon Series* and related issues.

As a special outreach to media ministry leaders, Intimate Life involves key broadcasters in Galatians 6:6 Intimacy Retreats.

If you know of a local broadcaster who would be interested in receiving Intimate Life programming, free-of-charge, or if your local group is in need of customized promotions and announcements for your own use, contact Mike & Jill Frazier through the Intimate Life Ministries office.

CHAPTER TWO
The Intimacy Message

The Intimacy Message: Part 1

God's Plan for Intimacy: Turning "Not Good" Into "Very Good"

Genesis is the book of beginnings. In the first few chapters of Genesis we witness God "setting up" His universe according to His sovereign design. An integral part of the creation process was the "birth of intimacy," revealed in the dilemma of Adam, the declaration of God, and His design for marriage, family and the church.

The Dilemma of Adam

"It is not good..."

In Genesis chapter one, on six different occasions, God observed His creation and commented that what He saw "was good." But in Genesis chapter two, after creating Adam, God made a startling statement. For the first time He said, "It is not good." And when God says something isn't good—it's not good!

Adam seemed to have everything he would need:

- ◆ Adam had a **perfect environment.** Adam was good—his mind was not corrupt, his heart was pure. Adam's circumstances were good—no pollution, traffic jams, or diseases; and he had a good job and no competition from others. His entire environment was unstained by sin.

- ◆ Adam **possessed everything.** He owned it all! No problems with daily provision, monthly salaries, the IRS, or retirement plans. Everything that God had created was his (Genesis 1:28-30)!

- ◆ Adam had an **exalted position.** He had dominion over everything created. He had no insecurities, jealousies, or pressure to perform. He was at the top of the ladder!

Let's pause to make an important observation. Adam had an exalted position, unlimited resources, and a perfect environment and yet it wasn't good enough. He had everything most people think is important, and yet if something didn't change, his Maker knew he wouldn't be fulfilled. Does this mean that if we achieved an exalted position—CEO, President, Superintendent, Chief, Senior Executive, Partner, Professor—we still might not be happy? Does this mean that if we accumulated unlimited resources—stocks, bonds, real estate, automobiles, houses—we still might not be fulfilled? Evidently so!

Our world tends to claim that the above three areas are what we need to live a fulfilling life. If we only had a more perfect job or spouse; if only we had a larger income or a bigger house; if only we had a higher position—

higher up on the ladder—then we would truly be happy! The lesson we learn from Adam is that he had all of these and yet it was "not good!"

It's also critical to note that even Adam's relationship with God was good—he walked and talked with his Creator; he had intimacy with God!

So what in the world was "not good" about Adam's situation? What was his dilemma? Apparently just one thing—Adam was alone.

A sovereign God, free to create Adam any way He desired, chose to fashion him in such a way that Adam needed to relate intimately to both God **and** other human beings. Adam's aloneness was a significant problem which had to be addressed. God had created Adam with needs—physical, emotional and spiritual needs—and Adam could not meet his own needs. They could only be met through meaningful relationships with God and others.

Adam was created with innate needs, and we have the same needs. Have you ever noticed how a newborn seems to have been created needing attention, affection, approval, and comfort? And these needs don't go away with age or maturity.

But why would God create us as "needy" humans? Perhaps it is so we would have to look beyond ourselves and trust God and His provision to meet our needs (Philippians 4:19). Could it be that this longing for intimacy with God and others is a key to understanding human motivation? Adam's dilemma seems to say—yes!

We all have needs, and we are motivated to have these needs met. If we're not careful, these needs can become so strongly felt, we'll succumb to one of three dangers:

The Danger of Self-Centeredness

"Do nothing from selfishness...think more highly of others" (Philippians 2:3).

Self-centeredness prompts a preoccupation with "taking" from another through manipulation, demands, and conditional love. The tragedy is that "taking" will never satisfy what God has created us to freely receive. Here's a scenario which illustrates the futility of the take/demand approach to having your needs met.

Wife – "You never spend time with me; you're always doing your own thing. This Friday night, could we go out for a date—just the two of us, without the kids?"

Husband – "You know I'm busier now at the office than I've ever been."

Wife – "What about this Friday?"

Husband – "I have an appointment..."

Wife – "I knew it!"

Husband – " All right...I'll rearrange it!"

Wife – "Oh, don't bother."

Husband – "Nope, you and me, Friday night, time alone."

Chances are, they'll go out together on Friday night, but the wife's need for attention won't be met because she had to demand that it be met. The husband wasn't giving out of a loving, caring heart; he merely acquiesced to the pressure he felt from his wife. A take/take relationship is devastating. A give/take relationship is frustrating.

A give/give relationship is satisfying.

The Danger of Self-Sufficiency

"You say , 'I am rich, increased with goods and have need of nothing' " (Revelation 3:17).

Relative to needs, some people don't think they have any; or, they acknowledge the fact that they have needs, but think they can meet them themselves. Either mentality leads to self-sufficiency.

Ironically, an attitude of self-sufficiency is often encouraged by two subtle but dangerous teachings that can be propagated by the church. The first one goes like this: "If you'll become spiritually "mature," you won't have any needs," or, "If you exercise 'real' faith, like me, you won't have any needs." The second sounds like this: "You don't need anyone but God to meet your needs. You should never need anyone but Him."

If we refuse to acknowledge that God may want to involve human relationships to meet many of our needs, three painful outcomes may occur: we may cut ourselves off from much of God's intended provision (We'll miss everything He wants us to receive from others.); we may minister judgment and condemnation to other "mere" humans who may rightly sense that they need other people ("What's wrong with you, just trust God."); and, if we think we don't need others, we may not realize that they may need us ("I don't need you, so why do you need me?").

The truth is, we do need each other! If we persist in our pride and self-sufficiency, God will resist us, and we'll miss out on the flow of His grace (James 4:6)!

The Danger of Self-Condemnation

"Therefore, there is now no condemnation for those who are in Christ Jesus" (Romans 8:1).

Self-condemnation is a subtle trap that says, "I know I have needs but I feel guilty because I do," or, "What's wrong with me—I'm lonely?" The truth is, if God created us with needs, then being needy can't be selfish! In our fallen state, we may behave selfishly, trying to "take" from others; if so, our sin is in the selfishness, not the neediness. Admitting we have needs is not a confession of wrong, it's an acknowledgment of our humanity and our "neediness" before God. It's realizing that we are "poor in spirit" (Matthew 5:3).

Even Jesus, the God/man, had needs. Jesus, as portrayed in the Gospels, was not only a sinless Savior, He was a person who expressed a need to relate intimately with His Father and with others.

So Adam's dilemma was his aloneness; he had been created with significant needs and there wasn't another human being with whom he could intimately relate. But God promised to solve Adam's dilemma...with His declaration!

The Declaration of God

"Therefore I will create for you..."

In Genesis 2:18 God declared that He would solve man's dilemma, and He did so by creating another human—someone with whom Adam could be intimate. God said, "I will make a helper suitable for him." Be assured—when God says, "I will"—He will!

The obvious and profound implication of this declaration is: we need each other! God never intended for us to live as hermits, nor does He expect us to be self-sufficient. Rather, He created us with needs; needs which can only be met within the context of meaningful relationships. Needs draw us together; needs are the catalyst for intimacy!

God determined that neither possessions nor position could satisfy our intimacy needs.

- ◆ A car is no substitute for affection.
- ◆ A house cannot meet our need for respect.
- ◆ Degrees and diplomas will not satisfy our need for love.
- ◆ A position of authority is not an alternative for comfort.

The deeply felt, God-given needs that we all have can only be satisfied by emotional and spiritual commodities, experienced through loving, deliberate, intentional giving by God and by other people.

- ◆ Only love can satisfy our need for love.
- ◆ Only affection will meet our need for affection
- ◆ Empathy is our source of comfort.
- ◆ Forgiveness produces peace.

God's Design For Marriage, Family and The Church

Adam not only needed to relate intimately with his Maker, but God created him with a need to relate intimately on a horizontal level with other people. Therefore God ordained three divine relationships: marriage (Genesis 2), the family (Genesis 4, Psalm 127:3), and the church (Matthew 16).

Since God's provision for our needs will often flow through marriage, the family, and the church, it shouldn't surprise us that our adversary (the Devil) will make every effort to steal, kill, and destroy these divine relationships (John 10:10). Just as surely as God says, "I will provide" through these three, Satan says, "I will seek to destroy them." Therefore we see:

◆ **Satan's attack on the first marriage** (Genesis 3), and his continued assault on marriages in our society. In America, 50% of all first marriages and 70% of all second marriages end in divorce; extramarital affairs are rampant; and surveys indicate that even among marriages that survive, many indicate a deep level of dissatisfaction (and this low level of marital satisfaction tends to be the same among church attending couples).

◆ **Satan's attack on the first family** (Genesis 4), and his continued assault on families in our society. In America, 2/3's of all children will spend part of their growing up years in a single parent home; child abuse seems out of control; and a recent national survey indicated that the typical American father spends only 14 minutes a week with his children—and 10 of those minutes are spent in discipline.

◆ **Satan's attack on the early church** (Matthew 16, Acts 4), and his continued assault on the body of Christ in the 20th century. The church in America is rocked by scandals and plagued with inefficiency, wrong priorities, lukewarmness, and worldliness.

But in the midst of Satan's attack on our marriages, families, and the church, Jesus still promises to give abundant life (John 10:10). Though Satan may rage, Jesus will provide a way of escape.

God has provided for our dilemma of aloneness by creating three "horizontal" or human relationships through which He could pour His provision and blessing.

These three divine relationships, on a horizontal level, have been ordained by God to minister to our "aloneness." Just as a "three-fold cord is not easily broken," God has graciously provided these three avenues through which His provision can flow. Marriage will not be for everyone but God can minister His love and comfort through family and the church. Marriages may break apart and families not function as intended, but the body of Christ can minister as God's "safety net" to meet people at their point of need.

A wonderful thing happens when, in the relational contexts of marriage, family, and the church, we joyfully give to meet the needs of others. We cooperate with the design of God and experience abundant living through intimate relationships.

The Apostle Paul speaks of the joy of relational intimacy in I Thessalonians 2:8-9, *"We loved you so much that we were delighted to share with you not only the gospel of God but our lives as well."* Intimacy involves this "sharing of one's life."

The perfect example of this sharing is Jesus, the God-man. Jesus demonstrated for us the need to live intimately with the Father (John 5:30) and the need to relate intimately with others. Notice:

◆ **Jesus had needs** – for air, food, and water, and He also needed comfort, companionship, and other "intimacy" needs.

◆ **Jesus communicated His needs** – *"My soul is overwhelmed with sorrow to the point of death. Stay here and keep watch with me"* (Matthew 26:38). Communicating need is a declaration of humility and faith.

◆ **Jesus experienced the pain of unmet needs** – *"Could you men not keep watch with me for one hour?"* (Matthew 26:40) He was a man acquainted with sorrows and grief, despised and forsaken (Isaiah 53:3). Jesus experienced the emotional pain of rejection, loss, disappointment and loneliness, so that He could be a great High Priest who can sympathize with our weaknesses (Hebrews 4:15).

◆ **Jesus received from others** as they ministered to His needs (John 12:1-6). When Mary anointed Jesus with costly perfume, the disciples rebuked this "extravagance," but Jesus received it without shame. Receiving from others demonstrates humility. When we refuse to receive from others, it's often an indication of our prideful self-sufficiency (remember Peter's initial refusal to have Jesus wash his feet [John 13:6,8]). Furthermore, without "receiving," there's no gratefulness, praise, or worship. Our receiving from others also underscores the message of Romans 8:32, *"He who did not spare His own Son, but gave Him up for us all—how will He not also, along with Him, graciously give us all things?"*

◆ **Jesus looked beyond others' faults and saw their needs** – Jesus never excused sin but He always looked beyond people's sin and saw their need. His unconditional love could separate a person's "worth" from their sinful behavior. In fact, He demonstrated His love toward us (declaring our worth) in that *"while we were still sinners, Christ died for us"* (Romans 5:8). In Luke 19 Jesus looked beyond the fact that Zacchaeus was a thief and liar, and He ministered to his needs: *"Come down immediately. I must stay at your house today"* (Luke

19:5). This ministry of agape love touches us deeply at our point of need and produces in us a heart-felt gratitude.

As these divine relationships function as God intended, we experience the intimacy of two becoming one in marriage (Genesis 2:24), the joy of children truly being gifts from the Lord (Psalm 127:3), and the church operating as one body (I Corinthians 12:27). Intimacy turns the "not good" of our aloneness into the abundance of "it is very good" (Genesis 1:31)!

God solved the dilemma of Adam by His great declaration and his wonderful design. It is — "God's Plan For Intimacy!"

In order for us to truly enjoy the satisfaction of intimate relationships as God has designed, we must recognize a specific prerequisite for intimacy. Let's now explore the second crucial element of the "Intimacy Message"— the importance of experiencing biblical truth.

The Intimacy Message: Part 2
Experiencing Biblical Truth: The Prerequisite for Intimacy

Jesus said, "You will know the truth, and the truth will set you free" (John 8:32). What does it mean to "know the truth?" Certainly there are concepts and ideas which must be grasped intellectually. But does "knowing" require more than intellectual assent?

A significant aspect of our "Intimacy Message" is that we must *experience* biblical truth in order to have the abundance of intimate relationships God desires for us. If we experience truth, then it impacts all three areas of our personality: our thinking, our behavior, and our emotions. When all three are affected, then we truly know the truth.

Romans 12:2 stresses the importance of "renewing our minds" according to truth as a normal aspect of our spiritual growth. So it's not surprising that intimacy in relationships can be greatly hindered by "faulty thinking." For example, if one spouse believes a lie like "Our problems are all your fault," and thus blames everything on the other partner, the couple will experience difficulty with intimacy — few of us want to draw close to someone who consistently blames us for all problems. Truthful thinking is thus a key "pathway" to experiencing intimacy.

James 1:22-25 clearly states that if truth does not affect our behavior, we don't really know it—that we must not be "hearers" only, but also "doers" of truth—we must put truth into practice. Thus we find that intimacy in relationships can be enhanced through the practice of "intimacy disciplines" such as weekly "Marriage Staff Meetings" and "Family Fun Nights." Intimate relationships don't happen by accident; intimacy-building behaviors enable people to draw closer to each other.

However, we must also observe that **"believing right" and "behaving right" are not enough to guarantee our experience of intimate relationships.** "Believing" and "behaving" are necessary, but not sufficient ingredients to bring about oneness in marriage, families, and the church.

What else is needed?

Living out biblical truth in relationships with God and others necessarily involves the world of human *emotion*. Expressing strong feelings with and for each other demonstrates sincere love: "Rejoice with those who rejoice, and weep with those who weep" (Romans 12:15). Comforting those who mourn is essential for emotional healing and subsequent experience of God's blessing (Matthew 5:4). In this manner, part of God's provision for healing is the genuine experience of emotional caring. Thus, the "imparting of our very life" to others who "have become so dear to us" (I Thessalonians 2:8) brings individuals, couples and families into the experience of true intimacy—the healing of deep hurt and the fellowship of great joy.

Conversely, emotional distance or "numbness" greatly hinders the experience of intimacy.

Jesus emphasized the importance of experiencing truth emotionally when He said we must love God with all our **hearts** as well as with our minds and strength. Joy and peace are integral aspects of a meaningful Christian life which we experience emotionally.

Too often, we have been content to simply "know about" basic tenets of our Christian faith. For example, we may be able to define the concept of confession, we may cite the appropriate verse for confession—I John 1:9— and we may even be able to quote the verse from memory. But do we really **know** what confession is? Have we experienced confession, not just as an intellectual concept, but also behaviorally and emotionally?

Let's continue with this example. What specifically is involved in experiencing confession? We would acknowledge that confession means agreeing with God and another about our sin, saying in effect, "I did it, and it was wrong" (Thought). We would actually say to God and whoever else we had offended, "I admit that I did _____ , and that was wrong" (Behavior). But very importantly, we would experience godly sorrow—a broken and contrite heart concerning our sin (Emotion). Our thoughts, behavior and feelings would all be involved in experiencing the biblical concept of confession.

Have we experienced confession in our most important relationships—with our spouses and our children? Our answer to this question highly correlates with the level of intimacy in these relationships.

Other critical aspects of Christian living which may lack this "experiencing" of truth could include:

> Forgiveness (I John 1:9, Ephesians 4:31-32)
>
> Comfort (Matthew 5:4; II Corinthians 1:3-4)
>
> Faith (Hebrews 11:1-6)
>
> Love "casting out" fear (I John 4:18)

Relationships within marriage, family, and the church are the contexts where biblical truth is to be "lived out" or experienced. Without this relationally experienced context, truth becomes simply knowledge that "puffs up" rather than love that "builds up."

◆　◆　◆　◆　◆　◆　◆　◆　◆　◆　◆　◆

Let's now explore the third key element in the "Intimacy Message:" God's concern for both our aloneness and our fallenness. This truth not only inspires deep gratitude within us, it also gives us a model for our ministries.

Intimate Life Ministries　23

The Intimacy Message: Part 3
God's Concern For Our "Aloneness" and Our Fallenness
(A Model for Ministry)

As we have seen, God placed Adam in a perfect environment, where he possessed everything, ruled everything, and had a relationship with God. Yet these gifts were not enough. God had created Adam in such a way that he needed even more of God's divine provision. Adam was still alone. God demonstrated that He cared about Adam's problem of aloneness by providing a solution to it: another human being like Adam who could then be God's channel to meet Adam's relational needs on a human level.

The point? *God cared about Adam's aloneness*; He was concerned enough about Adam's unmet needs for human relationship that He responded and did something about it.

Genesis 3 records the tragic fall of Adam and Eve into sinful rebellion. God had provided everything they needed physically, relationally and spiritually. Yet, in spite of these provisions, the man and woman violated the only limitation God placed upon them. Their disobedience represented not only a rejection of His commands, but also a rejection of Him and His loving provision.

How did God respond to their disobedience? Did he immediately strike them dead and start over again with someone else? Did He withdraw Himself from them, rejecting them as they had rejected Him?

Genesis 3:9 tells us that the omniscient God of the universe "called to the man, 'Where are you?'" Did God not know where Adam was?

These verses continue with God conversing with the man and woman, asking them questions. Did He not already know the answers to these questions?

God did pronounce judgment: they lost their perfect environment, their abundant possessions, and their exalted position. But God did not kill them nor did He reject them. Instead, He reached out to them in love, moving toward them even as they were hiding from Him.

Genesis 3:21 records God's desire to reconcile their relationship, even given the magnitude of Adam and Eve's sinful rejection of God: "The Lord God made garments of skin for Adam and his wife and clothed them."

Adam and Eve had lost everything, and they had no one to blame but themselves. Now they had a new need due to the shame of their nakedness. Their feeble attempt to cover their nakedness with fig leaves was inadequate. So God shed the blood of animals in order to provide for their need to cover their nakedness. In so doing God foreshadowed the shedding of the blood of His own Son in order to cover the sin of mankind, providing for our need of salvation.

The point? *God cared about them even in their fallenness.* He was concerned enough about their unmet need that He responded and did something about it, just as He had provided for them before they sinned.

What we see, not only with Adam and Eve but throughout Scripture, is God's concern for both people's aloneness and their fallenness. When Jesus encountered the notorious tax-gathering thief Zacchaeus (Luke 19:1-9), He did not immediately confront him with his dishonest behavior. Instead, He violated profound cultural and religious strictures against associating with such "riff-raff" by dining with Zacchaeus! He looked beyond Zacchaeus' faults and saw his needs for acceptance, attention, and love.

When Jesus came to the immoral Samaritan woman (John 4), He asked her for a drink of water and talked to her. He did acknowledge that her sin was an issue, but first He looked beyond her faults and ministered to her needs for acceptance, attention and love.

Thankfully, God does the same with us. **He is concerned about our sinful fallenness.** In fact, He is so concerned about it that He sent His Son to die on Calvary in order to pay the penalty of our sin. In addition, He has given believers the Holy Spirit in part to convict us of sin in our present lives. He then clearly tells us how we are to respond when we are convicted of sin: we are to agree with Him about it and receive His forgiveness and cleansing (I John 1:9).

And He is also concerned about our aloneness. He provides for the intimacy of fellowship with Himself through union with Jesus Christ, He in us and we in Him (I John 1:3; John 17:23). He even promises that He will always be with us (Matthew 28:20), never leaving us or forsaking us (Hebrews 13:5). And He also commands us to give to each other out of the abundance of His grace toward us.

Freely we have received...

- ◆ so He commands us to accept others (Romans 15:7).

- ◆ so He commands us to "carry others' burdens" (Galatians 6:2).

- ◆ so He commands us to respect others (I Peter 2:17).

- ◆ so He commands us to greet others affectionately (Romans 16:16).

- ◆ so He commands us to have concern for others (I Corinthians 12:25).

A significant aspect of our "intimacy message" is this: **Our ministries must reflect God's concerns: we must be concerned not only about people's fallenness but also their aloneness and unmet needs.** We can and should not only confront sin, but also seek to meet needs and minister to pain in the lives of others.

Hurting people will be drawn to our care and compassion. We will find that often we won't need to confront sin—that when we care for people's needs like Jesus cared for Zacchaeus, they often respond directly to God's gentle conviction of their sin, as they feel cared for and loved.

What might this look like in our own homes? If our spouse is slamming cabinet doors with an irritated facial expression, instead of firing off, "You know I can't stand you slamming cabinets! What's wrong with you now?!" we might say gently, "Gee honey, I can see you are upset about something . . . Would you like to tell me about it?"(Proverbs 15:1). To a child who is misbehaving because of not receiving attention, we might say, "Johnny, I see that you are upset. Let's spend some time together."

In our marriage ministries, we would urge an over-spending spouse to get finances under control, but we would also help the couple identify unmet emotional needs which might be contributing to the spending problem. We would admonish the adulterous spouse to stop the sinful relationship, but we would also encourage both parties to heal unhealed hurt that may in part have contributed to the adultery.

Essentially, we view a wide range of problems in living as symptoms not only of sin, but also of aloneness; thus, following the example of God Himself, we would be concerned about and seek to minister to both. We also seek to equip others to do the same as an indispensable element of intimate relationships.

CHAPTER THREE

An Intimate Life Ministry in the Local Church

Components of an Ongoing Intimate Life Ministry

Fortifying Our Homes, Churches, and Communities

When Asa became king of Judah, the country was in terrible condition morally and spiritually. King Asa immediately did what was good and right in the sight of the Lord, cleansing the nation of all immoral religious places and practices (II Chronicles 14:2-5).

He then determined to fortify the cities and towns of Judah while he had the opportunity, because they were not at war with anyone at that time. He knew that enemies would eventually return, so he had to prepare the cities for future battles. He declared to all the nation his gratefulness to God for the opportunity to fortify the nation: *"The land is still ours, because we have sought the Lord our God; we sought Him and He has given us rest on every side"* (II Chronicles 14:7).

Marriages and Families are His land!

Today, we have a similar challenge and a similar opportunity.

According to a recent Gallup poll, 73% of Americans reported often feeling lonely. The Institute for American Church Growth tells us that 78% of those new to church are there seeking ways to strengthen family ties. Josh McDowell's "Why Wait?" campaign found that 80% of teens and 86% of single adults desire help with relationships. According to research conducted by Josh McDowell's campus ministry, the # 1 long range goal of today's college student is "a happy marriage."

These statistics, combined with the assault on our marriages and families, challenge us to take advantage of any opportunity to "fortify" relationships against the enemies of individual isolation and family dysfunction and breakdown. We have the opportunity to equip people for relationships which provide security, refuge, and rest. What we need is not just the obvious "what to do," but also the practical "how to's" of intimate living with God and others.

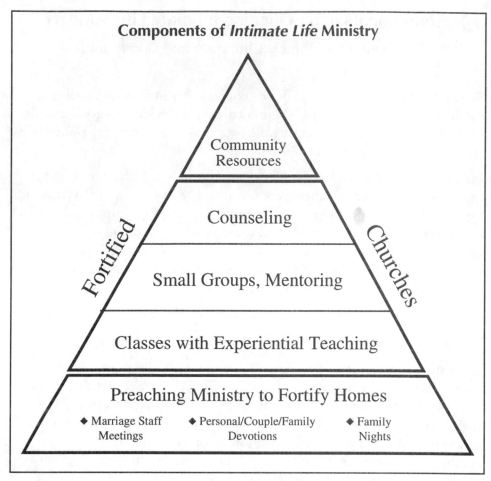

Components of *Intimate Life* Ministry

Fortified

Churches

Community Resources

Counseling

Small Groups, Mentoring

Classes with Experiential Teaching

Preaching Ministry to Fortify Homes

◆ Marriage Staff Meetings ◆ Personal/Couple/Family Devotions ◆ Family Nights

The above "pyramid" diagram represents various components of an *Intimate Life* ministry in a local church. The "class" level potentially involves larger numbers of people in "preventative" ministry. Higher up the pyramid, fewer people may be involved, but they often have a stronger commitment to doing homework and practicing principles. Also, the need for "corrective" help may be greater. Thus, more skill and training may be required of those who lead ministries in enrichment groups, mentoring, and counseling.

Let's look at these components in more detail:

Fortifying Homes

At least three practices have been found to greatly enhance marriage and family intimacy and satisfaction: couple "devotional" times, marriage "staff meetings," and "family fun nights." Churches are helping to fortify homes as the preaching ministry encourages couples and families to experience these intimacy building practices. The Intimate Life Sermon Series and the Intimate Life Newsletter are specifically designed to assist ministers with this challenge.

Couple "devotional" times: Husbands and wives can enhance their spiritual intimacy through focusing together on passages of scripture or other inspirational literature. Even briefly reading something together aloud and then praying silently provides meaningful spiritual enrichment which is shared and thus builds intimacy. A recent study indicated that only one out of 1014 couples who practiced regular devotional times together ended up divorcing. *Intimate Moments* was specifically written to facilitate daily couple devotional times.

Marriage "Staff Meetings:" Developing and maintaining marriage and family intimacy requires that a husband and wife spend quality time together. The external stresses of work, carpools, child raising, and checkbooks need not take their toll on marital oneness if couples take time to manage family events. No successful business operates without regular staff meetings, yet many families try to operate without a regularly scheduled time of planned communication where spouses are giving each other undivided attention.

Agendas for these meetings might include calendar coordination, family goal planning and progress assessment, parenting issues, vacation planning, talking and listening regarding whatever may be important at the time, sharing wishes, desires and dreams, giving each other productive feedback, and specifically expressing appreciation. (For further details, see the Special Edition No. 1 of the *Marriage and Family Intimacy* Newsletter, pages 13-14.) The *Intimate Encounters Workbook* and the *Parenting with Intimacy Workbook* provide specific topics and materials to cover.

"Family Fun Nights:" We often hear from older couples, "Enjoy your kids while you can; you won't always have them at home!" Is it possible to have quality time with our families where children are meaningfully involved, **not** around the television? Yes, and this time is essential for family intimacy, too. Start with one per month, then every other week, and then weekly. Consider letting each family member have a turn deciding what everyone will do for that evening. Ideas might include reading aloud from an exciting book, playing charades, going out for ice cream, working on an art or craft project, writing and reading poetry, acting out Bible stories, even a family talent show (video-taped for hilarious viewing later!). (For further ideas, see the Special Edition No. 1 of the *Marriage and Family Intimacy* Newsletter, page 7.) The *Intimate Family Moments Workbook* provides specific topics and materials to cover.

How One Church Helped Fortify Homes

The Pastor of a large Texas church recently determined to do something to strengthen and encourage couples in their marriages. He preached the "God's Plan for Intimacy" message, with a strong exhortation for couples to begin a daily devotional time, marriage staff meetings, and family nights. He then invited all who wished to make this commitment to come forward to receive the *Intimate Moments* devotional guide as a gift from the church. Over 500 couples responded!

As this example indicates, preaching the "God's Plan for Intimacy" message from the *Intimate Life Sermon Series* is an excellent way to fortify homes. These messages not only present biblical truth concerning intimate relationships, they provide the pastor opportunities to encourage congregations to begin these intimacy-building activities—both the "what to do" and the "how to do it."

Fortifying the Church

Not only can individuals, couples and families be strengthened through preaching and the encouragement of intimacy-building disciplines, entire churches can be fortified through a variety of ministry components.

Fortifying Churches Through Classes

A fortified church will consistently offer classes of various types where intimacy principles and practices are taught and modeled. Key to Intimate Life materials and training for class usage is the emphasis on "experiential teaching"— participants actually experiencing biblical truth in the class! Classes may be taught as part of a Bible teaching hour or as an elective during a non-Sunday morning time. Several churches are offering community marriage classes taught in neutral settings for outreach purposes, i.e., classes conducted at libraries, community colleges, YMCA, hotels, etc. Class series might be as short as four weeks or as long as sixteen weeks.

Classes have several advantages. Any number of people can attend. Discussion groups can be included in the format which provide for more personal experience of the intimacy principles. The "threat level" is low, allowing more cautious people to "warm up" to the concepts slowly. Intimate Life classes can be offered for all age groups and all types of relationships. Classes might be offered to teach pre-school children about humility and "neediness"; school age children might be led to explore the purpose of relationships, while teenagers explore principles of decision-making. Classes might be offered for college and single adults helping prepare them for meaningful friendships and relationships. Classes also might be offered for engaged couples, newly-weds, mid-lifers and empty nesters as well as the separated, single parents or the recently divorced. Parenting classes as well as family classes with parents, children and teenagers (in the same room!) could be offered. Perhaps most importantly, the visibility of such classes sends a strong message that relationships—with God and meaningful others—are important priorities of the church.

A disadvantage of the class setting is that participants typically are less committed to doing the "homework" (which is a vital prerequisite to experiencing genuine intimacy). Classes also "stir the pot"—they heighten awareness of needs and issues concerning marriage and family intimacy, and then identify people who want to go further with a higher level of commitment.

How Classes Have Helped Fortify Churches

In a North Carolina church, 80 young adults gathered on Sunday Morning to study *Top 10 Intimacy Needs*. The teacher presented concepts for 45 minutes; then for 30 minutes, participants discussed the principles and completed the "exercises" in table groups led by previously trained leaders. Thus, both large and small group experiences were provided in a Sunday Morning format.

An Oklahoma couple teaches *Intimacy Encounters* for 13 weeks once a year in its "Nearly-Newlywed" engaged couples class.

A New Braunfels pastor teaches *The Pursuit of Intimacy* as a community outreach ministry. Endorsed by the local newspaper and civic leaders, this 10 week marriage intimacy class meets in the local community center building and reaches couples from the surrounding area, many of whom do not attend church.

A Cleveland, Ohio area church helps prepare its single adults for intimate relationships using *Discovering Intimacy*.

An Arizona church brings older children, teens and their parents together each Sunday evening to share in family groups using *Intimate Family Moments*.

Numerous resources including books, study guides, audio tapes and videos are available to assist with Intimate Life classes. The *Ministry Orientation Kit* is a suggested first resource for churches interested in beginning an Intimate Life ministry.

Fortifying Churches Through Small Groups and Couple-to-Couple "Mentoring"

A fortified church will also consistently offer **small groups.** The "group" level will involve smaller numbers of people (perhaps 4-12) which will provide a setting within which intimacy principles can be explored in greater depth with discussion and support. Mutual encouragement and accountability are important aspects along with opportunities to "impart your very life to others" (I Thessalonians 2:8-9).

Groups for couples may include members of different age groups, neighborhoods, home fellowship groups, or they could be organized specifically for engaged couples, newlyweds, mid-lifers, or empty nesters. Intimate Life groups could also be offered for men, women, singles, families, the separated and recently divorced.

Participants typically meet for a specified number of sessions and also commit to completing the session's homework. This homework includes both individual preparation and couple or family activities. Thus, much of the real work and benefit occurs outside the group. Group time is spent with leaders teaching and modeling intimacy principles and members sharing benefits of their homework, asking questions and then experiencing together relevant biblical principles. These "essential" encounters with God's word are critical to the beneficial impact of these groups.

The advantages of a small group format include the opportunity for a higher commitment by the participants, and thus a greater accountability and support to follow through with those commitments. A high level of emotional support and comfort can also be provided to members as emotions such as hurt, fear and condemnation are encountered. Participants typically experience a depth of fellowship which is all too rare in many churches.

The main disadvantage for some people is that the group process can be too threatening, so a class environment might be recommended initially. Group involvement might also be difficult for couples seeking to overcome the damage of adultery or other serious offenses. Some couples may be dealing with a level of anger and other emotions too intense for many small groups.

The above disadvantages have led many churches to provide a special type of help: **a "mentoring" ministry.** The content and process of the mentoring relationship is very similar to the small group. The main difference is that a leadership couple works individually with another couple, individual or family. Sensitive information about the couple can be protected and troubled relationships that need more intensive help can receive what they need.

How *Intimate Life* Groups Have Helped Fortify a Church

A Texas pastor and his wife experienced a deepening of intimacy in their marriage through participating in an Intimate Life couples' marriage enrichment group. They decided to bring the benefits of this ministry to their church. Twenty couples, in four separate groups, agreed to work through the same material they had been through, with similar positive results. This church now offers these marriage enrichment groups along with groups and classes for singles and families in place of their Sunday Evening service. A leadership team of trained lay couples lead groups, supervised by the pastor and his wife.

The *Intimate Encounters Workbook* provides excellent group content for marriage enrichment/support groups. This workbook also provides everything necessary for couple-to-couple mentoring. The *Parenting with Intimacy Workbook* is used in parenting groups while the *Intimate Family Moments* devotional is used with family groups.

Single adults also need to learn better how to relate to others according to God's design for intimacy. *Discovering Intimacy,* a small group resource for singles who wish to explore intimacy principles and practices is being field-tested in various churches and is available from Intimate Life Ministries.

Many adults face the challenge of seeking to save or restore their marriage without the immediate involvement of their partner. Fortified churches can provide support for these adults in a small group format. *Restoring Intimacy: How to Save Your Marriage Alone* is a resource designed to meet this critical challenge. It is appropriate for both group and mentoring contexts and is available for church field-testing through the Intimate Life office.

The study guide, *Top 10 Intimacy Needs,* is an additional resource for group study and is being used in men's and women's groups, as well as with singles, couples and families. The *Heart Aflame* workbook and the book, *Spiritual Strongholds,* are important resources with a focus on deepening our intimate walk with God.

Fortifying Churches Through A Counseling Ministry

Most pastors regularly receive requests for counseling. A fortified church providing regular classes and groups will find that these ministries will increase the number of counseling requests. As the availability of Christ-centered relationship enrichment becomes known, referrals from the church and community will typically increase significantly. The church will increasingly feel the demand to provide counseling of some kind. Therefore, the development of trained, lay counselors is highly encouraged.

Because intimacy principles and practices are biblical, they apply to all relationships and relational problems and are transferrable to equipping lay leaders. Intimacy principles seek to address both current problems in living and their underlying causes. Individuals, couples and families are challenged to accept responsibility for their contributions to these problems and the hurt they have experienced is cared for and comforted. Unresolved pain from the past is addressed with special attention given to how present issues are affected. Counselees are consistently required to complete practical homework exercises.

Not only will intimacy principles assist the pastoral staff in their counseling duties, but key lay couples can be trained in this approach to counseling and can then help carry some of the counseling load for the local church.

How a Counseling Ministry Using Intimacy Principles Has Helped Fortify a Church

A church pastoral staff member was providing much of the counseling for his church in spite of the fact that his own marriage needed work. He and his wife were impacted by couple and group experiences with intimacy principles. This brought about significant emotional healing of their marriage pain and pain from their past. The pastor then began to apply these counseling principles in both group, individual, and couple counseling, with similar positive results, regardless of what the presenting problems were. He also began equipping the church's lay care-givers, so they could help carry the counseling load.

The *Intimate Encounters Workbook, Parenting with Intimacy Workbook, Discovering Intimacy, Restoring Intimacy,* and the *Intimate Life Newsletter* are also excellent counseling resources.

Fortifying the Church Through Community Resources

Every fortified church should have relationships with skilled community professionals. These professionals are important contributors to the security of fortified homes and churches. Individuals sometimes need medical, legal, financial, or counseling care which are beyond the scope of what even the strongest church can provide. These professionals can also provide consultation to church leaders facing difficult situations. It is especially helpful if these professionals have a thorough awareness of intimacy principles. This could be accomplished by participating in an Intimacy Institute program.

Fortifying Communities

A community would be considered "fortified" when enough fortified churches existed so that almost any member of that community could find a class, group, mentoring or counseling appropriate to their needs. In a larger city this may require one fortified church for every 10,000 population. Smaller communities can become fortified when enough churches of various denominations and ethnic composition are providing intimacy classes, groups, and/or counseling so that this ministry is accessible to everyone in the community. Intimate Life Ministries is committed to equipping local leadership through publications, leadership development conferences, media resources, and personal consultation.

◆　◆　◆　◆　◆　◆　◆　◆　◆　◆　◆　◆　◆

Intimate Life Ministries is committed to local, church-based intimacy ministries. No other oganization or agency can, will, or should do what the church is called to do.

In our next section, we'll consider some of the implications of recent research concerning how marriages, families and the church could make a profound difference.

Should Your Church Have A
Marriage and Family Ministry?
If Not The Church, Then Who?

◆ Several leading Christian professionals indicate that as much as 80% of a child's personality is formed by age 6.

– How is the church equipping parents of pre-school children to understand and guide the intellectual, emotional, moral and spiritual development of their child?

◆ Research consistently documents that by age 12, a child must have mastered three key developmental issues—compliant behavior, positive attitude, and daily responsibility—or life as an adult will be painfully problematic for the individual, the entire family and society.

– Rules without relationships produces/provokes rebellion.

– Should the church be bringing parents and families together for equipping concerning these three developmental issues?

◆ The highest church "drop out" rate is when the children of church families become teenagers and the family begins experiencing pain, embarrassment and guilt.

– Should the church be purposefully bringing together parents and their 12-14 year olds to focus on preventative skills covering communication, privacy, privileges, and rules?

◆ Pre-marriage testing using an instrument like "Prepare" is 80% accurate in predicting subsequent marriage stability or divorce.

– Since 75% of all marriages in America are conducted by ministers, should the church insist on pre-marriage testing and follow-up counseling prior to marriage?

◆ Several studies indicate that even a short 4-month mandatory "waiting period" between engagement and marriage with required classes, counseling or mentoring reduces the probability of divorce by 40%.

– Should the church participate in a community-wide marriage statement which offers these guidelines to couples seeking marriage prior to use of church facilities or ministers for weddings?

◆ Divorce statistics and marriage "scandal," seem to occur among church leaders and families as often as they do among the un-churched. This negative witness can be devastating to young believers and those outside the church.

- Should the church implement a practical marriage teaching and equipping ministry which would touch, over time, all married adults, plus a required married enrichment program for all leadership couples?

◆ Research indicates that teenage peer influence, whether "good" or "bad," cannot take the place of parental influence. In fact, without increased parental involvement during the sometimes difficult teen years, peer influence whether "good" or "bad" actually can undermine self-worth, heighten anxiety, and strengthen family alienation!

- Should church youth ministries be providing **both** an atmosphere of "good" peer influence and **purposeful family times** for vulnerability, skill development and resolution of inevitable conflicts?

◆ Studies documented and portrayed in popular books such as Gary Smalley's *The Blessing* consistently show that regardless of academic or athletic success, regardless of peer acceptance and exemplary behavior, children and teens hunger deeply for the parental blessing of affirmation. "You are my beloved son, in whom I am well pleased."

- Realizing this need and further considering the fact that many parents never received this "blessing" themselves, should the church be ministering to parents who missed it and equipping them to give it as they seek to establish a new heritage with their children?

- A functional family of origin is possible when both parents walk intimately with Christ, they have a healthy marriage, and are thus free to give to their kids.

◆ Developmental studies indicate that perhaps the most influential factor in any adult's success in a marriage relationship is the degree, depth and manner in which they have *"left father and mother"* (Genesis 2:24).

- Should the church be ministering in this area to families with older teens/young adults? Should this be a priority in college/singles ministry?

◆ Over 90% of all singles will marry and Gallup Surveys consistently show a "happy marriage" as their #1 dream with "feeling inadequately prepared" their #1 anxiety.

- Should the church create a safe and accepting environment in which crucial relational skills like vulnerability, trust, empathy, forgiveness and sharing the truth in love could be taught and experienced through support groups and mentoring?

◆ Over 78% of single-agains will re-marry. The divorce rate for second marriages is over 70%, often connected to unresolved issues and emotions from earlier relationships.

- Should the church prioritize a ministry of healing past hurts, helping people "recover" from past rejections and find freedom from common hindrances like guilt and condemnation?

◆ In 85% of all divorces, one spouse goes to great lengths to save the marriage even after separation, legal proceedings or finalized divorce.

- Given the declaration that "God hates divorce" and Paul's admonition to "remain single or be reconciled"—should the church establish a specific ministry to those who are trying to re-build or "save" a troubled marriage?

◆ Marriage stress and divorce rates are highly correlated with transitions in the marriage "life cycle" as couples move from having **no** children, to having children, to teenagers, to the empty nest, etc.

- Based upon this understanding, should the church develop specific ministries to couples in these **transitions** through support groups, mentor couples, etc. to help give guidance, encouragement and support?

◆ Over 70% of all children in America will spend some of their growing up years, in a single parent home—almost 30% rarely or never see one parent.

- Should the church play a particular role in ministry to these "half-orphaned" children and their parent through mentor families, adopt-a-dad programs, support groups?

Where Do We Go From Here?

Here are some practical steps to begin an Intimate Life Ministry in your church:

1. *Start with yourself:* your relationship with God, and your relationship with your spouse (if you are married).

   Every effective Intimate Life ministry in local churches is led by individuals and couples who have first experienced the benefits of these intimacy principles and practices. We should not attempt to share with others that which we have not experienced ourselves. What we freely receive, we then gratefully offer to others.

   A proven way to begin is to find three or four couples who desire to see their marriage intimacy deepened. These couples then commit to work through the *Intimate Encounters* workbook. If it is not possible to involve other couples, then work through it as a couple. In a similar way, a team of single adults could work through *Discovering Intimacy* together or a group of men or women could begin a small group study of the *Top 10 Intimacy Needs.*

2. *Participate in a Community Marriage Class and Intimate Life Training Workshop.*

   In several major cities in America and overseas, Intimate Life Ministries provides 8-week training sessions. These classes are taught by local pastors, regional coordinators and lay leaders. Couples and individuals who attend the classes experience intimacy principles by working through a particular Intimate Life resource and are also equipped in the "how-to's" of beginning an Intimate Life ministry in their local church. The syllabus for the community marriage classes is included in the next chapter. Similar training is being developed for the Parenting and Restoring Intimacy materials.

3. *Attend a Leadership Development Conference or a Regional Conference.*

   Several times a year in various locations, Intimate Life Ministries provides training for pastors, lay leaders, individuals and couples in various aspects of starting and developing a marriage and family ministry. In addition to overview general sessions, practical workshops are conducted to equip pastors and lay leaders to effectively conduct ongoing classes, groups and counseling ministry in the local church using intimacy principles. Call the Intimate Life office for a schedule of upcoming leadership development opportunities.

4. *Order a Ministry Orientation Kit.*

   This is the next best thing to attending a Leadership Development Conference. This excellent package of key Intimate Life resources will help you start an Intimate Life ministry in your church.

5. *Pastors: Preach "God's Plan for Intimacy" as a single message or a series of messages and challenge couples and families to begin regular devotional times, marriage staff meetings, and family nights*—providing the *Intimate Moments* devotional guide and the *Intimate Life* newsletter as follow-up resources.

   The *Sermon Series Kit* is a complete package including sermon notes, outline, background material, illustrations, and sample messages on tape.

6. *Senior Pastors: Attend a "Galatians 6:6" retreat with your spouse.*

   As an important aspect of fortifying communities, Intimate Life Ministries provides a specialized ministry to Christian leaders offering renewal, restoration, and equipping. These "intimacy retreats" for Senior Pastors and ministry staff couples are hosted in key cities throughout the United States and in other countries. See page 8 for more information.

The Multi-Dimensional Aspect of an Ongoing Marriage and Family Ministry

The breadth of Intimate Life ministry consists of five component parts. Each of the five components is essential in the development of a comprehensive marriage and family ministry and a ministry that encourages intimacy with God. Homes, churches, and communities will be fortified as each component is experienced through the "pyramid" of classes, small groups, and couple-to-couple "mentoring."

Intimacy with God: This component of the Intimate Life ministry seeks to help individuals realize that an intimate relationship with God is a prerequisite for intimacy with meaningful others. God is seeking worshippers and thus, individuals are encouraged to "bend" toward the Lord. In a variety of ways, individuals are led to understand, experience, and practice worship as their first priority.

Marriage Intimacy: This component seeks to help couples find freedom from the hindrances to intimacy as they come to experience the abundance that God intended. Couples learn to be vulnerable with feelings and intimacy needs, to give and receive affection, and share all of oneself. Through scriptural journaling, "marriage staff meetings," and group support, couples are led to experience a journey from pain to fulfillment.

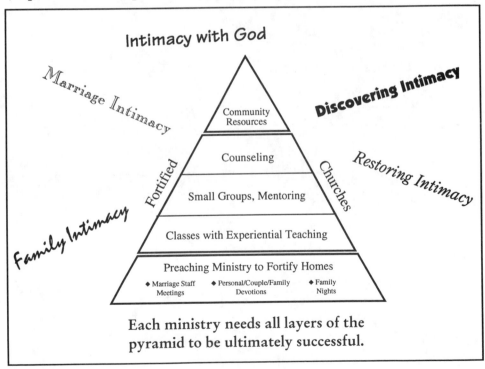

Intimacy with God

Marriage Intimacy

Discovering Intimacy

Fortified

Churches

Restoring Intimacy

Family Intimacy

Community Resources

Counseling

Small Groups, Mentoring

Classes with Experiential Teaching

Preaching Ministry to Fortify Homes

◆ Marriage Staff Meetings   ◆ Personal/Couple/Family Devotions   ◆ Family Nights

Each ministry needs all layers of the pyramid to be ultimately successful.

Family Intimacy: The parenting component emphasizes the right balance between love and discipline, rules and relationships. Parents are equipped to positively shape the emotional, intellectual, and spiritual development of their children. Families are brought together (parents, children and teens in the same room!) to learn how to establish home and family life as a place of refuge, strength and ministry.

Discovering Intimacy: This component of the ministry seeks to apply Intimate Life concepts and principles to older adolescents, college students and other single adults who wish to establish or enhance intimacy in their relationships. Single adults frequently need to invest substantial amounts of time developing close relationships in which they learn to *"impart their very life"* to others (I Thessalonians 2:7-8). Through scriptural journaling and group discussion, single adults are led to experience truly intimate relationships with God and others.

Restoring Intimacy: A key component of this ministry targets one partner in a relationship who is seeking to save the marriage "alone." It equips the willing partner with restoration skills helpful in reconciling with the other partner in the relationship. Through scriptural journaling, "restoration encounters," and group support, an individual is equipped and supported as they seek to re-engage his/her partner in the intimacy journey. An additional component of this ministry seeks to promote healing from relationship breakdowns, failures and losses (divorce recovery, grief and abuse issues).

CHAPTER FOUR
Leadership Training Opportunities

Community Marriage Class and Leadership Training

Intimate Life Ministries sponsors eight week community marriage classes and Intimate Life training courses. They are usually offered in major cities in the fall and spring. The classes consist of 1-1/2 hours of training in intimacy principles (usually using the *Intimate Encounters Workbook*) and thirty minutes of instruction on how to use the material to begin an Intimate Life Ministry in the local church.

The classes are taught by ILM Regional coordinators, pastors, or trained laypersons. A synopsis of the eight week training program is given on the following pages.

Community Marriage Class and Leadership Training
Week 1

Topic

1. Intimacy – Definition and Assessment
   Resources - Chapter 1 of *Intimate Encounters,*
         Chapters 1 and 5 of *Pursuit of Intimacy*

2. Concept of "fortifying" families
   Daily Devotional
         Intimate Moments
         Special Newsletter - page 5

   Marriage Staff Meetings
         Special Newsletter - page 13
         Intimate Encounters - Chapter 16

   Family Nights
         Special Newsletter - page 7
         Handout

Key Scripture

"For this reason a man will leave his father and mother and be united to his wife, and they will become one flesh" (Genesis 2:24)

Group Discussion

1. Have everyone in the group introduce themselves and share this information: Men - Name, how long they've been married, where they work, their hobby.

   Women - Name, something about their family, their hobby.

2. Ask this question (not everyone needs to respond) - "Why did you sign up for this workshop?" or, "What do you hope to get out of this workshop?"

3. Ask this question - "What is intimacy?"

4. Emphasize that this is a *workshop.* It will be very important for everyone to do his/her homework.

5. Choose several of these different aspects of intimacy and discuss how they would positively impact a marriage relationship. Then discuss the opposite of each of the characteristics and consider how it would negatively impact a marriage relationship.

Openness, honesty, mutual self-disclosure, caring, warmth, protecting, helping, being devoted, mutually attentive, mutually committed, surrendering control, dropping defenses, becoming emotionally attached, feeling distressed when separation occurs.

Assignment

1. Read "Maintaining Healthy Relationships" (page 6 in the Special Newsletter) and be prepared to discuss the three key Scriptures in your group next week.

2. Have a Marriage Staff Meeting, Daily Devotionals, and schedule your first Family Night. Be prepared to share your progress in these three areas next week.

3. Complete Chapter 1 of the *Intimate Encounters Workbook*.

Intimate Life Leadership Training

Pages 1-7 of the *Intimate Life Ministries Handbook.*

1. What is Intimate Life Ministries? – Pages vii-viii

2. The mission of Intimate Life Ministries – Pages 3-7

Assignment - Read pages 15-26 in the Handbook by next week.

Community Marriage Class and Leadership Training
Week 2

Topic - Intimacy Needs

1. God's Plan for Intimacy

   Resource - Special Newsletter

2. Commonly Identified Intimacy Needs

   Resources - *Top 10 Needs Booklet*
   Chapter 2 – *Intimate Encounters*
   Chapters 3 and 4 – *Pursuit of Intimacy*

Key Scriptures

"It is not good for man to be alone" (Genesis 2:18).

"And my God will meet all your needs according to His glorious riches in Christ Jesus" (Philippians 4:19).

Group Discussion

1. Review last week's assignment.

   Having read "Maintaining Healthy Relationships," discuss these questions:

   — How do you handle conflicts in your marriage; do you tend to "stuff" your feelings or "spew" them? How does Ephesians 4:15 address this issue?

   — Do you "put-off" dealing with hurts and misunderstandings? What does Ephesians 4:26 teach regarding confronting problems?

   — How are we to respond to someone who verbally attacks us? (Proverbs 15:1) What might a "soft answer" sound like?

   ◆ Ask, "How was your Marriage Staff Meeting?" "Were you able to have at least one devotional together?" "Have you scheduled a Family Night?"

   ◆ Ask, "What did you learn from taking the two Intimacy Assessment surveys?" (from chapter 1 of *Intimate Encounters*)

2. Relative to intimacy needs:

   ◆ Do you realize you have these needs?

   ◆ Do we ever outgrow these intimacy needs?

◆ How does it make you feel when you think about having these needs?

Weak? Guilty? Selfish? Embarrassed?

Why do you feel this way?

◆ What attitude would we have about our needs?

3. Consider again the exercise on page 12 of *Intimate Encounters:*

◆ How accurately did you assess your spouse's needs?

◆ How similar/different were the most important needs of you and your spouse?

◆ What do the answers to the 2 questions reveal?

◆ Are our "most important needs" likely to change throughout our life?

Assignment

1. Complete Chapter 2 of *Intimate Encounters.*

2. Have a Marriage Staff Meeting, Daily Devotionals, and plan a Family Night.

Intimate Life Leadership Training

Pages 15-26 of the *Intimate Life Ministries Handbook.*

The Intimacy Message:

Part I. God's Plan for Intimacy - Pages 15-21

Part II. Experiencing Biblical Truth - Pages 22-23

Part III. God's concern for our "aloneness" and our fallenness - Pages 24-26

Assignment – Read pages 29-40 in the Handbook by next week.

Community Marriage Class and Leadership Training
Week 3

Topic

    1. The Pain and Potential of Intimacy Needs

        Resources - Chapter 10 of *Intimate Encounters*, Chapter 7 of *Pursuit of Intimacy*

    2. Emotional Cup

        Resources - Chapter 3 of *Intimate Encounters*, Chapter 7 of *Pursuit of Intimacy*

Key Scripture

"And my God will meet all your needs according to His glorious riches in Christ Jesus" (Philippians 4:19).

Group Discussion

    1. Review last week's assignment.

        ◆ Answer this question, "When do you feel most loved and cared for by your spouse?"

        ◆ How did your Marriage Staff Meeting go? Were you able to have a devotional together? Have you had a Family Night?

    2. Relative to emotional needs being neglected, what would be the potential outcome if these needs were neglected in childhood?

        Comfort   Approval   Encouragement   Security

    3. Relative to emotional needs being lovingly met, what would be the potential outcome if these needs were lovingly met in childhood?

        Attention   Respect   Affection

    4. If the following needs are being neglected in a marriage relationship, how might the neglect be expressed in a negative way? Compose some sentences that would allow a partner to "speak the truth in love" as they share their neglected needs.

        Attention   Respect   Affection   Security

Assignment

1. Complete Chapters 3 and 10 of *Intimate Encounters*.

2. Have a Marriage Staff Meeting, Daily Devotionals together and a Family Night.

Intimate Life Leadership Training

Pages 29-40 of the *Intimate Life Ministries Handbook*.

Discuss the importance of beginning the Intimate Life "triangle" (page 30) ministry with a strong **marriage** intimacy ministry:

◆ Involving classes, small groups, mentoring, etc.

◆ Followed by the addition of:

Parenting with Intimacy - for parents and families

Discovering Intimacy - for single adults, college and older teens

Restoring Intimacy - for the separated, divorced, abused, etc.

Intimacy with God ministry

Why would beginning with a strong **marriage** intimacy ministry be so important?

Community Marriage Class and Leadership Training
Week 4

Topic

    1. Speaking the truth in love.

        Resources - Chapter 16 of *Intimate Encounters*, page 6 of Special Newsletter

    2. Confession and Forgiveness

        Resources - Chapter 4 of *Intimate Encounters*, Chapter 9 of *Pursuit of Intimacy*

Key Scriptures

"Speak the truth in love" (Ephesians 4:15).

"If we confess our sins, He is faithful and just and will forgive us our sins" (1 John 1:9).

"Therefore confess your sins to each other and pray for each other so that you may be healed" (James 5:16).

"Forgive each other, just as in Christ God forgave you" (Ephesians 5:32).

Group Discussion

    1. Review last week's assignment.

      ◆ How did your Marriage Staff Meeting go? Were you able to have a devotional together? Have you had a Family Night?

      ◆ Relative to unmet needs producing unproductive behavior (see diagram on page 117 of *Intimate Encounters*), can you identify in your own life how unmet needs might be causing some unproductive behaviors?

    2. Discuss the parable of "the log and the splinter" in Matthew 7:1-5. How is this parable applicable to the forgiveness/confession process between spouses? Which is easier to see, how your spouse has hurt you or how you have hurt your spouse? How do you go about removing the log from your own eye?

    3. Why are we reluctant to confess and forgive? Is it possible to genuinely forgive others unless we have been forgiven by God (and have accepted His forgiveness)?

    4. Instead of confessing our sin we often blame others, offer excuses, offer a flippant confession, or ignore the sin. "Play out" the above four "substitutes" in the following two scenarios. What might John and Cindy be tempted to say as substitutes for genuine confession?

- Having promised his wife that he would be home at 5:00 o'clock for a special evening together, John gets home at 7:00.

- Cindy blows up at her husband because he forgets to take out the trash.

What would a proper confession from John and Cindy sound like?

Assignment

1. Complete Chapter 4 of *Intimate Encounters*.

2. Have a Marriage Staff Meeting, Daily Devotionals together, and a Family Night.

3. Begin working on the "Key Elements of an Intimate Life Ministry in the Local Church" handout (page 67 of the Hnadbook).

Intimate Life Leadership Training

Intimate Life Training Resources for an Ongoing Ministry.

1. Marriage Intimacy Ministry

- Class packet
- Small Group packet
- Counseling packet

Initial Curriculum:	*Intimate Encounters Workbook, Pursuit of Intimacy Book, Intimate Moments Devotional.*
Follow-up Curriculum:	*Top 10 Intimacy Needs, Lies We Believe Workbook, Healing Power of Intimacy,* and *Thinking Straight to Intimacy.*
Other Resources:	*Parenting with Intimacy Book, Parenting with Intimacy Workbook, Intimate Family Moments, Design for Family Intimacy, Discovering Intimacy - for single adults, college and older teens, Restoring Intimacy - for the separated, divorced, abused.*

Community Marriage Class and Leadership Training
Week 5

Topic

1. Freedom from Fear

   Resources - Chapter 6 of *Intimate Encounters*, Chapter 9 of *Pursuit of Intimacy*

2. Leaving and cleaving

   Resources - Chapter 11 of *Intimate Encounters*, Chapter 11 of *Pursuit of Intimacy*

Key Scriptures

"There is no fear in love. But perfect love drives out fear" (l John 4: 18).

"For this reason a man will leave his father and mother and be united to his wife, and they will become one flesh" (Genesis 2:24).

Group Discussion

1. Review last week's assignment.

   ◆ How did your Marriage Staff Meeting go? Were you able to have a devotional together? Have you had a Family Night?

   ◆ How was your time of confession and forgiveness?

2. Thinking back on some areas of your relationship in which you had to confess to your spouse and ask his/her forgiveness, what areas do you now expect to change? How do you expect to be different? (Godly sorrow brings about repentance.) An example of this would be:

   "I had to confess to my wife that I have not been supportive of her in the area of raising our children. I'm going to start helping get the kids to bed on time, help with their homework and be the primary disciplinarian."

4. In your family of origin:

   ◆ How was conflict handled?

   ◆ How did your family give attention?

   ◆ How did your family show affection?

   How have these three factors affected you and your marriage?

Assignment

1. Complete Chapters 6 and 11 of *Intimate Encounters*.

2. Have a Marriage Staff Meeting, Daily Devotionals together, and a Family Night.

Intimate Life Leadership Training

Page 67 of the *Intimate Life Ministries Handbook*.

1. Continue working on the "Key Elements of an Intimate Life Ministry in the Local Church" handout.

2. Discuss "Fortified Communities" – page 37.

Community Marriage Class and Leadership Training
Week 6

Topic

1. Mourning and Comforting

    Resources - Chapters 7 and 12 of *Intimate Encounters*, Chapters 11 and 12 of *Pursuit of Intimacy*

Key Scriptures

"Blessed are those who mourn, for they shall be comforted" (Matthew 5:4).

"The Lord heals the brokenhearted and binds up their wounds" (Psalm 147:3).

Group Discussion

1. Review last week's assignment.

    ◆ How did your Marriage Staff Meeting go? Were you able to have a devotional together? Have you had a Family Night?

    ◆ After reflecting on the "leaving and cleaving" principle, how well have you "left" your family of origin?

2. What does mourning/grieving sound like? What does comfort sound like? Why are we reluctant to mourn? When people need comforting, what do we often give them instead (possible answers include - pep talk, instruction, and criticism)?

3. How could the principle of mourning/comforting be applied to raising children? How we relate to our colleagues and friends? In counseling?

4. Are men more reluctant to mourn and grieve than women? Why? Why are some men insensitive to their wives when their wives are mourning?

Assignment

1. Complete Chapters 7 and 12 of *Intimate Encounters*.

2. Have a Marriage Staff Meeting, Daily Devotionals together, and a Family Night.

Intimate Life Leadership Training

1. Using the "Key Elements" guide (page 67), develop a personalized plan and strategy to begin your marriage intimacy ministry; visit this week as needed with pastor, other church leaders, etc...

2. Discuss "Where To Go From Here?" – pages 41-42.

Community Marriage Class and Leadership Training
Week 7

Topic

1. Four Ingredients of Intimacy

    Resources - Chapter 5 of *Intimate Encounters,* Chapter 6 of *Pursuit of Intimacy*

Key Scriptures

"Let nothing be done though selfish ambition or conceit, but in lowliness of mind let each esteem others better than himself" (Philippians 2:3).

"Freely you have received, freely give" (Matthew 10:8).

Group Discussion

1. Review last week's assignment.

    ◆ How did your Marriage Staff Meeting go? Were you able to have a devotional together? Have you had a Family Night?

    ◆ Were you able to experience the blessing of the "comforting and mourning" principle as it relates to childhood hurts and losses?

    ◆ Did you have the opportunity to comfort anyone this past week? Did you have a need to mourn this week? If you did, was your mourning met with comfort?

2. Relative to the four ingredients of intimacy:

    ◆ When do you feel "cared for" the most?

    ◆ Do you have a difficult time communicating vulnerably? If so, why?

    ◆ What do you enjoy doing together as a couple?

    ◆ Why is a give/give relationship better than a take/take relationship?

3. Why is the order of the four ingredients important? Caring, trusting, needing, giving.

4. Match the four ingredients of intimacy with these four hindrances to intimacy - fear, unresolved anger, selfishness, self-sufficiency. (Which ingredient is most likely to be affected by fear?)

Assignment

1. Complete Chapter 5 of *Intimate Encounters*.

2. Have a Marriage Staff Meeting, Daily Devotional together, and a Family Night.

Intimate Life Leadership Training

1. Finalize your personalized plan (pages 67-68) and turn in.

2. How can the three Hebrew words for intimacy be applied to marriage, parenting and church pastors? – pages 141-142

3. Discuss the Multi-Dimensional Aspect of an Ongoing Marriage and Family Ministry (pages 43-44).

Community Marriage Class and Leadership Training
Week 8

Topic

Overview of remaining chapters.

1. Emotional expression, emotional responding

Resource - Chapter 8 of *Intimate Encounters*.

Synopsis

Most of us were never taught how to communicate our emotions or how to respond properly to other people's feelings. Without developing an adequate "vocabulary" to express feelings, most adults enter marriage hopeful of deep emotional closeness but unable to achieve it. We must also learn how to appropriately respond to emotional expression, that is - emotional expression should be answered with emotionally responding.

Group Discussion

1. Write down as many emotions as you can. Why is our "emotional vocabulary" usually limited?

2. Emotional responding means that when emotion is expressed by one person, an emotional response is given in return. Explain how these four types of responses might be used as "substitutes" for true emotional responding: logic or reasoning, criticisms, complaints, neglect.

2. Emotional Games

Resources - Chapter 9 of *Intimate Encounters*, Chapter 10 of *Pursuit of Intimacy*.

Synopsis

We all have important intimacy needs such as attention, affection, comfort, and support. But rather than reveal our true needs and feelings to God and our partner, we often find it easier to play emotional games. When these unproductive responses are not stopped, they form patterns of behavior called "marital games."

Group Discussion

Here's a brief description of six common marital games. Create and "act out" each game.

1. "Complainer" vs. "Procrastinator" - This game typically begins with one partner making a request. The spouse agrees to the request but doesn't follow through. After asking over and over with no results, the first spouse becomes the complainer, while the other postpones fulfilling the request and becomes the procrastinator.

2. Nothing's Wrong - A classic way to draw attention to unmet needs without being vulnerable is to play the "nothing's wrong" game. This game can be portrayed by facial expression, body language, attitude, or behavior.

3. Blame Game - This game is played in order to avoid personal responsibility for one's own actions. By diverting attention to your partner's behavior, rationalizing your own becomes much easier.

4. "Performer" vs. "Yes, but..." - This game is common among couples who engage in power struggles. One partner may give a suggestion and the other quickly shoots it down. One partner initiates and the other tentatively agrees but eventually is oppositional.

5. "Outdone" vs. "Sweet Martyr" - This game is often initiated by the spouse who is overwhelmed by his/her own neediness. Almost every conversation is turned back toward Sweet Martyr's needs, while the hapless, helpless partner is "outdone" in every way as his/her own needs, hurts, and desires are minimized or ignored.

6. "Frustrated" vs. "Never Enough" - The Never Enough game begins with the message, "If you'll only do this for me, ...I'll be satisfied." But the Never Enough partner is not satisfied; he or she always finds something else to complain about. This leaves the other partner frustrated!

3. Thinking Straight

Resources - Chapter 13 of *Intimate Encounters*, Chapter 8 of *Pursuit of Intimacy*, "Thinking Straight to Intimacy" booklet.

Synopsis

How we *think* eventually controls how we feel, how we act, and eventually who we are; so it's important to think straight! In time, we can develop unhealthy "thinking patterns" - habit patterns of the mind which negatively affect our lives and relationships.

Group Discussion

Here's a brief description of six common unhealthy thinking patterns. Which patterns do you suffer from?

1. Personalizing - This thinking pattern causes one to think that life events are personal rejections and attacks. "Personalizers" tend to be moody and easily hurt by so-called rejections. Filled with insecurities, they develop low self-esteem and may blame themselves for everything.

2. Magnifying - This thinking pattern makes "mountains out of molehills." "Magnifiers" may be volatile with anger, unmerciful with self-condemnation, or "bottomless" with self-pity. Their vocabulary often includes words like: devastated, worst, ruined, terrible, horrible, awful.

3. Overgeneralizing - This thinking pattern insists that "history always repeats itself." Overgeneralizers rely on past events to predict the future and usually carry around lots of anxiety, doubt, and fear.

4. Emotional Reasoning - This thinking pattern causes one to interpret feelings as factors. Regardless of evidence to the contrary, "emotional reasoners" are convinced that if they feel a certain way, it must be so.

5. Polarizing - "Polarizing" is a perfectionistic thinking pattern that views life as all-or-nothing, good-or-bad, black-or-white. They tend to hold to rigid rules for evaluating life.

6. Selective Abstracting - This thinking pattern tends to focus exclusively on a few negative traits to the exclusion of positive ones.

4. Establishing a Vision for Your Marriage

Resources - Chapter 14 of *Intimate Encounters,* Chapter 14 of *Pursuit of Intimacy,* and *Strategic Living.*

Synopsis

Proverbs 29:18 states that, *"Where this is no vision, the people perish."* Marriages will benefit from systematic goal-setting because it provides a basis for oneness, offers a framework for decision making, is a reminder of important priorities, provides a sense of accomplishment and security, and it is an example and witness to others.

Group Discussion

1. How does Amos 3:3 relate to goal setting?

2. What is the difference between short-range, medium range, and long-range goals? Think of some sample goals (using all three dimensions of time) in each of these areas - financial, spiritual, personal, educational, family, marriage, professional, personal/social.

5. Stages of Marriage Intimacy

Resources - Chapter 15 of *Intimate Encounters,* Chapter 15 of *Pursuit of Intimacy.*

Synopsis

Marriages go through predictable stages. Understanding these stages helps explain the constantly changing demands and expectations of family interaction. Being aware of these stages helps us to be prepared for the inevitable challenges and stresses accompanying them.

Group Discussion

Here's a brief description of the four stages of marriage.

1. New Love - The honeymoon begins and two individuals start blending their lives together.

2. Shared Love - The first child arrives and love must now be shared.

3. Mature Love - The first child becomes a teen and love had better be mature!

4. Renewed Love - The last child is launched into the real world and love can now be renewed!

What are some of the challenges you would expect in each stage? What are some of the positive benefits of each stage?

6. Intimacy Disciplines

Resources - Chapter 16 of *Intimate Encounters,* Chapter 14 of *Pursuit of Intimacy.*

Synopsis

In order for a good marriage to remain healthy, couples must constantly "fine tune" all areas of intimacy. Intimacy can be preserved and enhanced through the regular practice of "intimacy disciplines" such as Marriage Staff Meetings, dates, learning to share the truth in love, expressing appreciation, emotional responding, and the cultivation of the physical relationship.

Group Discussion

1. If you and your spouse met privately for 1 1/2 hours each week, what could you talk about that would be beneficial to your marriage and family?

2. How long has it been since you and your spouse went on a date alone?

Intimate Life Leadership Training

Gather together in groups of 2-3 couples to pray together for the launching of your *Intimate Life* ministry.

Key Elements of an Intimate Life Ministry in the Local Church

1. Key Personnel
   Staff Liaison _____
   Director of Ministry _____
   Secretary _____

2. Pastoral Support of Ministry
   Attend Galatians 6:6 _____
   Attend Regional Conference _____
   Attend a Training Session
       1 day Leadership Development Conference
       8 week Community Marriage Class and Leadership Training
   Preach Sermon Series _____
   Host an Intimate Life Leadership Development Conference ____
   _____

3. Lay-Leadership Couples (Current and Potential)
   _____   _____   _____
   _____   _____   _____
   _____   _____   _____

4. Challenge to Fortify Families
   Date Sermon Preached _____
   Public Announcement of Intimate Life Ministry _____
   Number of Special Newsletters Needed _____
   Number of *Intimate Moments* Needed _____

5. First Teaching Class
   Teacher _____
   Group Leaders? _____
   Date and Time _____
   Location _____
   Means of Promotion _____
   Intimate Life Resources to be Ordered _____
   _____
   _____

6. Enrichment Groups
   Leaders _____
   Topics _____
   Date and Time Started _____
   Location _____
   Intimate Life Resources to be Ordered _____
   _____

7. Mentoring Couples
   Potential Couples _____
   Couples Confirmed _____
   Training Scheduled _____

8. Lay/Pastoral Counseling
   Potential Counselors _____
   Counselors Confirmed_____
   Training Scheduled _____

9. Professional Counseling
   Community Resources_____

10. Representation of Intimate Life Ministry in Budget
    Potential Line Items: Resources, Counseling, Training/Conferences,
    Publicity/Printing, Galatians 6:6.

11. Community Involvement (Fortified City)
    Regional Coordinator _____
    Other Participating Churches _____
    Public Conferences _____
    Training Opportunities _____
    Media Involvement _____

12. Recruiting Another Church for an Intimate Life Ministry
    Identify Church _____
    Plan to Approach _____

13. Outreach to Community _____
    Class/Workshop _____
    Direct Mail to Newlyweds/New Divorce Filings _____
    Counseling Services _____

Intimate Life Network
Referral Form

Committed to Help Fortify your Church and Community Against Such Enemies as Divorce, Abuse & Teenage Rebellion

"Providing a place of refuge, security and rest" (II Chronicles 14:2-7).

Please fill in all information:

Church/Ministry Name _____

Street Address _____

City _____ State _____ Zip _____

Telephone _____ Fax _____

Sr. Pastor/Ministry Director _____ Spouse's Name _____

Telephone _____

Staff Contact _____ Spouse's Name _____

(if different than Sr. Pastor)   Telephone _____

Lay Coordinator _____ Spouse's Name _____

(in addition to Staff Contacts)   Telephone _____

Please indicate below in which of these areas you are using *Intimate Life* materials:

Our church offers: ☐ Classes   ☐ Pastoral Counseling   ☐ Pre-Marital Counseling

☐ Support/Enrichment Groups   ☐ Marriage Preparation Training

☐ Lay Counseling/Mentoring   ☐ Divorce Recovery Ministry

☐ Separation/Reconciliation Ministry   ☐ Other_____

☐ I would like more information on the Galatians 6:6 Ministry

☐ Please send invitations to the following ministry friends for the Galatians 6:6 Ministry:

	Name	Church	Address	Phone
1.				
2.				
3.				
4.				

Completed by _____ Telephone _____
             (please print)

_____ *Intimate Life Ministries*   69

Hosting an Intimate Life Leadership
Development Conference In Your Church

Objectives:

1. Launch or expand an Intimate Life Ministry in your church and community.

2. Train and equip church leadership in Intimate Life principles.

3. Minister to marriage, family and other needs in your church.

4. Outreach to unchurched in your area.

5. Potential funding source for expanded marriage and family ministry (see information under Specific Host Church Responsibilities).

Format:

Friday: 6:30 pm - 9:30 pm   Intimate Life Training

Saturday: 8:30 am - 4:30 pm   Intimate Life Conference

Two-Day Conference (Fri/Sat)
Focus on church staff and lay leadership
Cost for lay leadership: $25 per person – special rate available for Host Church

Saturday Only Conference
These sessions are open to your congregation, other churches and the public.
Cost: $25 per person - special rate available for Host Church

General Host Church Requirement:

1. Minimum of 200 paid registrations from your church and community

2. Provide facilities to accommodate approximately 200 on Friday and 400 on Saturday

3. Promote conference to other churches

Specific Host Church Responsibilities:

7 months prior	Church returns conference scheduling form - then receives conference planning packet.	$500 conference scheduling deposit (will be applied to registrations)
6 months prior	Sr. Pastor/Clergy couple attend Galatians 6:6 "Get-Away"	Ministry gift from CMFI (Church pays for travel only)

5 months prior	Church Leadership Team (4-6 couples) work through *Intimate Encounters Workbook*	Order at reduced cost from CMFI
4 months prior	Church begins implementation of conference promotional plan	Ministry gift from CMFI
3 to 1 month prior	Pastor shares "God's Plan for Intimacy" sermon	Ministry gift from CMFI
	– Challenges church members to begin daily devotions, Marriage Staff Meetings, and Family Nights	
	– Inaugurate Intimate Life Ministry	
Conference Date	Church hosts conference in accordance with Implementation Plan	

Other responsibilities of Host Church:

1. Provide Registration Coordinator to receive registrations and to be listed in publicity materials.
2. Provide facilities for conference (including cost of utilities, janitorial support, etc.).
3. Promote the conference in Host Church as you would any church-wide emphasis - i.e., Missions Conference, Revival, Bible Conference, etc.
4. Intimate Life Ministry Team serves as Host Church Steering Committee.
5. Provide nursery as needed/desired.
6. Coordinate local promotion through other pastors, churches, and ministries.

Leadership Development Conference Request

Church or Organization: _____

Address: _____

Phone: _____ Fax: _____

Contact Person: _____

Workshop Desired: Please Specify

Note: Before hosting a Parenting, Thinking Straight or Healing Power seminar you need to have had been through the Marriage Intimacy first.

Marriage Intimacy – Speakers:	Intimate Life Ministry Staff
Parenting with Intimacy – Speakers:	Dr. Paul Warren and Terri Ferguson
Thinking Straight to Intimacy – Speaker:	Dr. Chris Thurman
Healing Power of Intimacy – Speakers:	Dr. Robert Hemfelt and Jim Walter

Any of the above

Desired Date(s) of the workshop:

     1.

     2.

The workshop attendees will consist of:

     1. The above church or organization only.

     2. Several churches and organizations in the area.

     3. Other (please specify) _____.

Estimated attendance at the workshop: _____

Return to:

Intimate Life Ministries
P.O. Box 201808 ◆ *Austin, Texas 78720*
(512) 795-0498 ◆ *(800) 881-8008* ◆ *Fax (512) 795-0853*

Intimate Life Regional Coordinators
Bi-Annual Planning Meeting With Intimate Life Network

Concept:

Twice a year (July-August and January-February) each Regional Coordinator couple hosts a meeting with all the coordinators from the Intimate Life Network in their region. Each church should be represented. Hopefully the local church coordinator couple will attend but if they cannot, *they need to send another couple.*

Example — If there are 30 churches in a region who have an Intimate Life ministry, all 30 churches should be represented at this meeting.

Also, churches/couples can be invited to attend the meeting who do not currently have an Intimate Life ministry in their church but would like to begin one.

Where and when is the meeting held?

This is up to each Regional Coordinator. The meeting could be on a week-night, a Saturday morning, or over lunch. Allow for about 2 hours. It could be held at a church, in a home, or a neutral location.

What do you talk about?

1. Quick update from each ministry about what they have going in their church/community.
2. Introduce new resources from Initimate Life Ministries.
3. Discuss new strategies for local churches to use (example: Intimate Life Sunday School class).
4. Plan Intimate Life training/growth strategy for community.
   - When is the next Community Marriage Class and Leadership Training Class? Where?
   - Do we (region) want to host an Intimate Life Saturday conference? If so, which one (Marriage, Parenting, Healing, Straight Thinking?), where, when, etc. If so, how can we guarantee 200 registrants?
   - Do we (region) want to host a Regional conference? If so, where and when? How can we guarantee 400 registrants?
5. Strategize marriage/family policies for the community (ex. pre-marriage policies, divorce laws, etc.).
6. Enlistment of other churches who could begin an Intimate Life Ministry.
7. Update regarding national ministry of Initimate Life Ministries (regional conferences, radio/TV opportunities, etc.).
8. Pray for your region that it will become "fortified."

CHAPTER FIVE

Key Elements in the Development
of an Intimate Life Ministry

Worship, Our First Priority

Using the *Heart Aflame* Resource to Develop Intimacy with God Through Worship

I. The Priority of Worship

A. Threefold purpose of the New Testament church - Exalt God, edify the saints, evangelize the lost. Is there a priority to these three?

B. Scriptures to consider when determining priorities: Matthew 22:36-38, Luke 10:38-42, John 21:15-17.

II. Defining Worship

A. Key words - English-weorthscipe, Hebrew-shaha, Greek-proskuneo.

B. Worship is the expression of a love relationship.

III. The Pathway to Worship

A. *"Enter His gates with thanksgiving and His courts with praise"* (Psalm 100:4).

B. There is a difference between thanksgiving, praise, and worship.

IV. Characteristics of Worship

A. Worship's scope

B. Worship's uniqueness

C. Worship's direction

V. The Profile of a Worshipper

A. "The acceptability of any act of worship is determined by the acceptability of the worshipper." Ron Dunn

B. Key verses relating to the importance of preparing the heart for worship: Matthew 5:8, Hebrews 12:14, Psalm 15:1-2, Psalm 24:3-5, Matthew 5:23,24, Mark 7:6-8,13

VI. The Therapeutic Aspect of Praise

A. Praise gets our focus off ourselves and others and onto God.

B. We become transformed into the image and character of that which we worship.

C. In God's presence we are reminded of His great love for us, His forgiveness, and His acceptance.

D. A life filled with praise will be joyful, merry, and cheerful.

Overcoming Spiritual Strongholds
Living Victoriously in Christ

I. What is a Stronghold?

A. The progression of sin: sin, besetting sin, foothold, stronghold.

B. Characteristics of a stronghold.

II. How are Strongholds Established?

A. Through unconfessed sin.

B. Through habitual, presumptuous sin.

C. In hardened hearts.

D. Through parental influence.

III. How to be Set Free from Strongholds

17 Steps to Freedom

IV. Twenty Four Spiritual Strongholds

Detailed analysis of these 24 strongholds: bitterness, rebellion, worry, greed, laziness, uncontrolled speech, gluttony, lying, sexual immorality, corrupt music, addiction, anger, unbelief, pride, fear, despair, worldliness, wrong self-image, selfishness, jealousy, apathy, religious bondage, impatience, and pessimism.

Hearing God
Maintaining Intimacy with the Creator

1. The Kind of Intimacy

   ◆ Everyone has access to the Father and an intimate relationship with Him. He loves us; He actually likes things about us. He wants to talk to us more than we want Him to talk to us.

   ◆ True spiritual food is not listening to sermons and tapes, or reading books or even the Scriptures. Spiritual food is the personal words of God to each of us.

2. Our Part in Intimacy

   ◆ Intimacy with God involves opening up our hearts to God in all truthfulness -NO MASKS. He knows what we're feeling anyway; we can't hide anything from Him. He wants to hear us say that we are angry, sad, frustrated, happy, etc. We can come to Him ready to hear instructions for the day.

3. Our Part in Listening to Abba Father

   ◆ God made us to be communicators. Hearing is done with the heart, not the ears. We get to know Him personally and experientially.

   ◆ Recording our conversations with God in a journal has several benefits:

      a. It is easier to pay attention - it keeps our minds from wandering.

      b. You have God's words to you in black and white.

      c. It gives expression to impression. He speaks to us in a still, small voice. If we squelch His voice we will lose our ability to be impressed by Him.

4. The Results of Real Intimacy

   ◆ We experience true intimacy by living it out in our daily lives. The Holy Spirit guides us into "all truth." Truth is the reality that lies behind appearances. It is lived out in our lives when we love our spouse, our children, and when we get along with our neighbor.

   ◆ God is always sure. When He gives us daily instructions and we live them out, He always comes through exceedingly abundantly.

   ◆ God goes with us wherever we go because He is in us. His number is not 911. His number is an 800 number, free to us anytime, anywhere.

   ◆ The most important thing in life is to experience an intimate love relationship with our Father.

Developing an Intimate Relationship
with a Sovereign God

I. The Old Testament Temple was Modeled After God's Design of Mankind

A. The Outer Court - Body - World Consciousness – "soma"

B. The Holy Place - Soul - Self Consciousness – "psyche"

1. mind

2. will

3. emotions

C. The Holy of Holies – Spirit – God Consciousness – "pneuma"

II. The Three Basic Parts of the Human Spirit Corresponds to the Ark of the Covenant in the Temple Holy of Holies — Each Part Must be Cultivated

A. INTUITION: God revealed Himself and His will through the law. Today, God reveals His will to the believer's intuition. *"Immediately Jesus knew in His spirit what they were thinking in their hearts"* (Mark 2:8).

B COMMUNION: God manifested His glory and received man's worship at the mercy seat. Today, those redeemed by Christ have their human spirit regenerated and worship and commune with God in their inner spirit. *"Yet a time is coming and now has come when the true worshippers will worship the Father in spirit and truth, for they are the kind of worshippers the father seeks. God is spirit and His worshippers must worship in spirit and truth"* (John 4:23-24).

C. CONSCIENCE: The ten commandments were kept inside the Ark. As the two tablets accused or excused the Israelites, the conscience is designed to guide Christian conduct. *"I speak the truth in Christ — I am not lying, my conscience confirms it in the Holy Spirit"* (Romans 9:1).

III. Keep the Spirit Clean: Sin Impairs the Ability of the Spirit to Know God
Ephesians 4:30: *"Grieve not the Holy Spirit of God who is within you."*
Matthew 5:8: *"Blessed are the pure in heart for they shall see God."*
I Thessalonians 5:19: *"Quench not the Holy Spirit of God who is within you."*

IV. Confession is God's Method for Cleansing a Dirty Spirit
"If we confess our sins He is faithful and just to forgive our sins and to cleanse us from all unrighteousness" (I John 1:9).

V. Pray in the Spirit as Well as in the Soul (I Corinthians 14:14)

VI. God Invites Us to Draw Near to Listen to Him
Exodus 20:18–20 shows us that God speaks to us in a number of ways; but best of all He has provided a spiritual organ that, when cultivated, is most dependable of all: intuition in the human spirit.

But be careful. God's voice is not the only voice that speaks.

Dividing spirit and soul is essential in understanding who is speaking to us!
Hebrews 4:12-13 — God speaks in the spirit. Self and/or Satan speak in the soul.
Discerning which is which is a matter of long-term cultivation.

VII. How Can We Distinguish Between God's Voice and What May Be My Voice or Satan's Voice?

Now Comes The Crisis: Will We Live by the *Spirit* or by the *Soul?*

Developing a Comprehensive Intimate Life Ministry in the Local Church

Does your church have an "ongoing" marriage and family ministry? Most churches have an annual emphasis on marriage and family but do not have ministry opportunities available year round. There are countless Christians sitting in the pews Sunday after Sunday knowing that they should have a healthier marriage and family but not knowing how to achieve that goal. They feel ill equipped, frustrated, hopeless and guilty!

Insightful Statistics

 ◆ Several studies indicate that a short 4-month mandatory "waiting period" between engagement and marriage, during which the engaged couple attends marriage classes and counseling, cuts divorce by 40%.

Does your church offer premarital counseling or classes?

 ◆ As marriages progress through the transitions associated with the marriage "life cycle," (couples move from having no children, to having children, to teenagers, to the empty nest, etc.), stress in marriage and divorce become more probable.

Does your church have ongoing ministries to assist couples through these transition times?

 ◆ Over 78% of single-agains will remarry and the divorce rate for their second marriage is 70%. This high rate is directly connected to unresolved issues and damaged emotions from earlier relationships.

Does your church offer ministries that help single-agains heal past hurts and learn new skills to avoid further broken relationships?

Good News!

You can start now and resources and training are available! If training and resources were not available, you would feel much like the Christian in the pew who knows he should have a healthier marriage but not know where to begin.

Churches all over the nation have begun "ongoing" marriage and family ministries! Here are a few examples:

 ◆ Young Adult Study - On Sunday mornings, 90+ young adults gather to study the *Intimate Encounters* workbook during the Bible study hour.

 ◆ "Empty Nest" Group - on Tuesday evenings, a home group works through intimacy principles with a particular focus on couples facing the challenges of the empty nest.

◆ Enrichment Groups – on Sunday evenings, 16 couples are taught a new intimacy principle each week and then break up in groups of four couples to discuss their homework and staff meetings from the *Intimate Encounters* workbook.

A Startling Reality!

Many cults and heretical groups have been formed throughout history because the church has not been effective in reaching people at their point of their key needs. One of the greatest needs that every person has is the need for meaningful relationships. The local church should be assisting people in developing intimate relationships with God, their spouses, siblings, and brothers and sisters in Christ. Through these intimate relationships, they will experience the abundance that Christ offers.

What Does an Ongoing Marriage and Family Ministry Look Like?

◆ Leadership - everything rises and falls on leadership. Your church needs you to start the spark of marital and family renewal. You are not expected to be an expert or to have "arrived" when it comes to your marriage and family. We are all on a journey. The main quality that you must possess is striving to walk your talk and apply these intimacy principles to your life.

◆ Class Setting - teach intimacy principles in a classroom type setting. This class could be taught in a school, bridal shop, Sunday School class, worship service, church training time, community center or wherever is best for your situation.

◆ Enrichment Groups - principles of intimacy are shared on a deeper level among four to six couples. These couples complete the *Intimate Encounters* workbook or other Intimate Life materials. There is meaningful group empathy and greater accountability!

◆ Mentor Couples - this is when one couple meets with one other couple on a regular basis and discusses intimacy principles. Mentor couples have been through the materials before and help other couples through barriers that they may face.

◆ Counseling Help - counseling training can be provided by your church in intimacy principles including staff and/or lay couples. A referral list of community resources could also be developed and given to appropriate caregivers.

Challenging Marriages and Families
from the Pulpit

Our American culture is groping for new definitions of the family—and of man/woman relationships! It is hard to follow God's standards in a country of increasing adultery, cohabitation, and lesbian/gay revolutions. What a wonderful opportunity! More than ever before people are looking for real answers and real help. The Christian church can provide a plan for marriage and the family which will work. This workshop will focus on principles which produce solid, stable, nurturing family settings—and some creative methods to communicate those truths from the pulpit.

I. Pulpit Preaching Must Focus in Three Broad Areas in Today's Culture.

   A. Marriage Must Develop the Relationship Between the Husband and the Wife (Ephesians 5:1 8-33).

   1. A Spirit-Filled Foundation is Essential (5:18-21).
      In order to fulfill the divine pattern for the family, the participants must be Christians! In order to fulfill the divine pattern for the family, the participants must be Spirit filled! Disobedient and fleshly Christians will have discord in the family.

   2. Mutual Submission Must Occur Between the Husband and Wife (5:21-24). Read Philippians 2:1-11.
      This model only works when the husband is more faithful in his love (5: 25-33) than the wife is in submission (5:22-24).

   3. The Love of the Husband Must be All-Encompassing (5:25-33).
      The husband's headship is modeled after Christ. The husband is not the head as an autocrat but as a servant: *"For the Son of Man has come not to be served, but to serve"* (Mark 10:45).

      The Husband's Duty is to Love His Wife (5:25) Love is something you DO!

      The Husband's Love is to Be:

      a. Unconditional-Sacrificial Love (5:25)

      b. Purifying Love (5:26-27)

      c. Caring Love (5:28-30)

      d. Unbreakable Love (5:31)

B. Blended Families Mix Complex and Diverse Relationships.
One in every four children in this country lives in a "blended"
family. If the trend continues to the year 2000, families with
stepchildren will outnumber families raising their own children. The term "blended family" is the label for the home that
is putting two families together. Perhaps a more correct title
would be "blending families." This indicates a constant,
ongoing process. It will always have its ups and downs.

There does not seem to be one blended family in the Bible
that worked well!

1. Blended Families Have Two Extra Stressors God Never
Designed.
   a. Someone else's Ex!
   b. Someone else's child!

2. Here Are Some Suggestions for Helping People Develop Healthy Blended Families.
   a. Clarify expectations (Proverbs 3:13-20)
   b. Mourn the losses (2 Samuel 12:15-25)
   c. Build a team (Philippians 2:1-2)
   d. Strengthen your marriage (Ephesians 5:21-33)
   e. Help the children heal (Matthew 18:1-6)
   f. Work hard at conflict resolution (Matthew 5:25-26)
   g. Agree on discipline (Proverb 13:24)
   h. Build a strong relationship with God and other
      believers (Galatians 6:2)
   i. Practice agape love and forgiveness (John 13:34-35)
   j. View your step-parent role as a ministry
      (Matthew 18:5)
   k. Don't be in a hurry for success (Philippians 4:6)

When we stop to think about it, everyone who has received
Jesus Christ as Lord and Savior is being blended into the
family of God.

C. Parenting Must Develop a Distinctively Christian Home
(Ephesians 6:4; Deuteronomy 6:4-8).

1. God's Truth Must be Imprinted on Our Children's
Hearts (Deuteronomy 4:4-6).
When Jesus Christ is upon our hearts, it won't be too
long until Jesus Christ is upon our children's hearts.

2. God's Truth Must be Deeply Imprinted in our Homes
(Deuteronomy 6:7).

Notice that imprinting is accomplished by the verbs, "impress," and "talk." "Impress" involves both teaching (Proverb 22:6) and discipline (Proverb 29:17).

"Talk" implies normal every day life, conversation, modeling, and behavior.

3. God's Truth Must Become a Habit in the Lives of Our Children (Deuteronomy 6:8). "Christian parenting is infilling children with the Word of God and the life of God so that they will always respond in a predictable manner." (Craig Massey's Definition of Christian Parenting)

4. A Righteous Child is the Product of Show and Tell.

II. New Methods are Needed to Communicate the Principles to Today's Culture.

A. The pastor's family is a powerful source of illustration, but only if certain conditions are met.

B. Today's visual learning society demands that preaching communicates like never before.

C. What are the tools for better communication? How can we implement them?

The Zacchaeus Principle

He Looked Beyond My Faults and Saw My Needs

In Luke 19:1-9, the gospel writer, Luke, records the beautiful story of Zacchaeus' conversion experience. Zacchaeus cheated people on their taxes. Zacchaeus was put in the camp with "sinners" in his community (v. 7). The people where Zacchaeus lived wouldn't associate with him and seemed to write him off as someone who would never change. However, Jesus, looked beyond his faults and saw and met his needs. The results were spectacular! Zacchaeus experienced salvation through faith in Christ and changes in his behavior were immediate! Zacchaeus cried, "Look, Lord. Here and now I give half of my possessions to the poor, and if I have cheated anybody out of anything I will pay back four times the amount."

Key Question – If Jesus would have simply rebuked him for his behavior and not gone to Zacchaeus' home, would the results have been the same?

Jesus Christ used his discernment to determine why people act the way they do. Jesus realized that people often behave in certain ways because of unmet needs in their lives. Have you ever stopped to wonder why:

- ◆ a husband stays long hours at work night after night
- ◆ a wife is irritated when the house is not spotless
- ◆ a child is having a fit over which clothes to wear
- ◆ a young boy feels he has to be the class clown
- ◆ someone escapes into drugs, pornography, etc.

Most of the time, people behave the way they do because of met or unmet needs.

Zacchaeus needed attention but tried to get it in sinful ways. People would probably yell and complain to him or beg him to be fair. This was not healthy but he was getting the attention he desired. Zacchaeus was small in stature and may have always felt self-conscious about his height. He probably felt big whenever he utilized his power as a tax collector. This may have helped meet his need for acceptance.

Does this mean our sinful actions are justified by our unmet needs? The answer is no, never. A painful past and unmet needs are not to be used as excuses for sinful behaviors. However, the Zacchaeus principle teaches us that when God given needs are met in our lives, this empowers and motivates us to do what is right and healthy and not what is wrong and harmful.

Another Key Question – Is it OK to have needs as a Christian?

If we are ever going to change our destructive behaviors or minister to someone so that they can change their actions, we must start by admitting that we do have needs and that is OK.

In Philippians 4:19, the apostle Paul says, *"And my God will meet all your needs according to His glorious riches in Christ Jesus."* If God said that we have needs, it must be all right to have needs. What are some of the needs of a child ?

- ◆ Affection
- ◆ Approval
- ◆ Attention
- ◆ Comfort

Does a child grow out of these needs? No! As adults, we still need hugs and kisses, someone to ask us how we are feeling, someone to affirm the work we do and to appreciate us and comfort us when we are hurt by others or circumstances.

When our needs are met by God through His Spirit, His Word, His people and our parents and spouses, we are then empowered and motivated to do what is right!

When our needs go unmet, we often react by participating in sinful behaviors because of the frustration that we experience.

Consider the following formulas:

Needs Met = Fulfillment   *Needs Unmet = Frustration*

Another Key Question – How could the Zacchaeus principle impact your approach to all people?

- ◆ As a parent
- ◆ As a friend
- ◆ As an employer/ee
- ◆ As a church member
- ◆ As a minister

Emotional Responding

Key to Relational Closeness

Emotional Responding is learning to respond to another person's emotions. If your spouse, child or friend expresses an emotion, you need to answer him/her with an emotional response. It would sound something like: "I know you are hurting and I care; I know you have a need and I care."

This is often very difficult for us to do because:

1. We grew up without a feeling vocabulary.

2. We won't let our hearts feel what our heads know.

3. It is easier to answer emotions with unproductive responses.

4. We have no idea what emotional responding looks or sounds like. In order to enhance your marital relationship, let's take a look at these four points and learn how to effectively apply them to any relationship.

  I. Developing a feeling vocabulary.

    A. As children, if you were not taught to name your feelings and express them, then you probably entered into adulthood unable to communicate those same feelings to others (like your spouse or children).

       1. You might have even hoped they could guess how you feel and respond appropriately.

       2. But how can they identify your feelings and emotions if you can't give them a name?

    B. Using a chart like the one on page 82 of *Intimate Encounters,* learn to identify feelings and give them names.

 II. Learn to let your heart feel what your head knows.

    A. In order to experience abundance and intimacy we have to open up to feelings.

       1. We are wired to think, feel and do.

       2. Many of us don't handle the feeling part well.

    B. Jesus experienced emotion.

       1. He wept at Lazarus' death – John 11:35.

       2. In the upper room He wanted His joy to remain full in the disciples – John 15:11.

       3. In the garden His soul languished unto death – Matthew 16:38.

C. Jesus experienced emotions but He did not let them control Him.

D. It is OK for me to experience emotions - that does not make me weak.

III. Unproductive responses.
Emotion should always be answered with emotion. Many times we answer with other things and they never work.

A. Facts, logic and reasons – Your best friend has just said some hurtful words to you. As you tell your husband about it he responds, "Don't let what she says bother you, you know it isn't true."

B. Criticism – Or he responds, "You sure are sensitive. Why do you let her get to you so easily? You really need to toughen up."

C. Complaints – "It sure was stupid to let all those people know how easily she gets to you. I found the whole thing embarrassing. If you keep this up we won't have any friends."

D. Neglect – "Well, I sure hope you can work it out. It's not my problem."

IV. What does emotional responding look and sound like?

A. It always includes understanding, empathy, gentleness, reassurance and confession if necessary.

B. If your wife is hurting how does that make you feel? (sad, compassionate, etc.)

1. Use those feeling words to communicate to her how it makes you feel to see her hurting: "It saddens me to see you hurt because I care about you; I have compassion toward you when you hurt because I love you."

2. Look at your wife, move toward her, hold her hand and tell her you love her.

C. When we put productive responding into practice we experience Matthew 5:4.

1. A person is hurting – Mourning

2. Someone comforts them – Comfort

3. The hurting person receives – Blessing, even when nothing external has changed. The thing that hurt may still be in place—but I'm "blessed" that you care!

D. Comforting is powerful.

   1. God tells us to weep with those who weep – Romans 12:15.

   2. God tells us to comfort others with the same comfort that we have received – II Corinthians 1:2-4.

   3. God tells us it is not good for man to be alone – Genesis 2:18.

V. Practice emotional responding in the following situations. Be careful not to answer with logic, criticism, complaints, or neglect.

   A. You come home from work. The house is a mess and so is your wife. You can see she is visibly upset. You say _____.

   B. Your wife (child or close friend) says, "I don't think Ann likes me anymore." You answer _____.

   C. Your husband comes home complaining that he is burned out, there's not enough time to accomplish all he needs to do. You answer _____.

   D. Your spouse (or child) communicates that you don't spend any quality time together anymore. How will you respond?

   E. You and your spouse had a special evening planned and you got held up at the office. What will you say when you get home?

   F. Your in-laws are coming to visit uninvited. This always causes a great deal of stress in your spouse. What will you say?

VI. Learn to tell your spouse what you need in this area of emotional responding.
Tell him/her what you need and don't need before you ever share the hurt.

   A. "I need to talk about something that's bothering me. Could you just sit with me and listen. I don't especially need any answers. Maybe just your arm around me and if I get emotional, reassure me that you care."

   B. This alleviates the fear of not knowing what to do.

If Christ Were Your Counselor

What Jesus Would Say to Life's Pain

A. Christ wants to be your counselor and is completely competent to be so.

1. I Kings 22:5 – *"First seek the counsel of the Lord."*

2. Psalm 16:7 – *"I will praise the Lord, who counsels me."*

3. Psalm 74:24 – *"You guide me with your counsel, and afterward you will take me into glory."*

4. Isaiah 9:6b – *"And he will be called Wonderful Counselor, Mighty God, Everlasting Father, Prince of Peace."*

5. Isaiah 28:29 – *"All this comes from the Lord Almighty, wonderful in counsel and magnificent in wisdom."*

B. The goal of Christ's counseling is to reproduce Himself in us.

1. Romans 8:29 – *"For those God foreknew he also predestined to be conformed to the likeness of his Son."*

2. Ephesians 4:13 – *"Until we all reach unity in the faith and knowledge of the Son of God and become mature, attaining to the whole measure of the fullness of Christ."*

C. The primary characteristics of Christlikeness include:

1. Unconditionally, Sacrificially Loving
John 15:13 – *"Greater love has no one than this, that one lay down his life for his friends."*

2. Selfless Servant
Matthew 20:28 – *"Just as the Son of Man did not come to be served, but to serve, and to give his life as a ransom for many."* John 6:38 - *"For I have come down from heaven not to do My will but to do the will of Him who sent me."*

3. Righteous
Hebrews 4:15 – *"For we do not have a high priest who is unable to sympathize with our weaknesses, but we have One who has been tempted in every way, just as we are-yet was without sin."*

4. See Reality Exactly As It Is
John 14:6 – *"Jesus answered, 'I am the way, the truth, and the life.'"*

5. Responsible
He didn't blame people for His own feelings and actions and didn't let others blame Him for theirs.

6. Free
   Galatians 5:1 – *"It is for freedom that Christ has set us free."*

D. Christlikeness is produced by The Work of God + The Word of
   God + Personal Commitment + Other Believers + Time and Trials:

   1. The Work of God– God does His job of regenerating us,
      teaching us His truth, disciplining us when we sin
      Philippians 2:13 – *"For it is God who works in you to will
      and to act according to his good purpose."*

   2. The Word of God – Necessary for knowing God, ourselves,
      and how to live life
      II Timothy 3:16-17 – *"All Scripture is inspired by God and is
      profitable for teaching, for reproof, for correction, for train-
      ing in righteousness, that the person of God may be ad-
      equate, equipped for every good work."*

   3. Personal Commitment – We do our part by studying
      Scripture, praying, fellowshipping with other believers, etc.
      Psalm 1:1 – *"Blessed is the man who does not walk in the
      counsel of the wicked or stand in the way of sinners or sit in
      the seat of mockers. But his delight is in the law of the Lord,
      and on His law he meditates day and night."*

   4. Other Believers – We need the support, encouragement, and
      challenge of others
      Proverbs 27:17 – *"As one man sharpens iron, so one man
      sharpens another."* Hebrews 10:24 – *"And let us consider
      how we may spur one another on toward love and good
      deeds."*

   5. Time and Trials – Maturing in Christ is a process that takes
      time and involves going through difficult situations
      James 1:2-4 – *"Consider it pure joy, my brothers, whenever
      you face trials of many kinds, because you know that the
      testing of your faith develops perseverance. Perseverance
      must finish its work so that you may be mature and com-
      plete, not lacking anything."*

E. If Christ were our counselor, He would work on:

   1. Helping us see ourselves as we really are.

   2. Helping us make internal changes versus external, cosmetic
      changes.

   3. Helping us not fit into the world.

   4. Helping us stop blaming others for our own "stuff."

   5. Helping us get real with others.

6. Helping us renew our minds with the truth.

7. Helping us love others and ourselves.

8. Helping us find peace in a sovereign God.

F. The issue of taking appropriate responsibility is a tough one for all of us.

1. We are, by nature, finger pointers.

2. The problem of blaming others goes all the way back to the Garden of Eden.

3. There are three main ways we fail to take appropriate responsibility:

   a. We take too much responsibility (neurotic)

   b. We take too little responsibility (character disorder)

   c. We bounce back and forth between doing both.

4. The challenge is to take responsibility for your own thoughts, feelings, and actions and not take responsibility for other people's thoughts, feelings and actions.

5. The failure to take appropriate responsibility greatly hurts individuals, marriages and families.

Overcoming the Lies We Believe

A. The Bible emphasizes "straight thinking" in life.
Philippians 4:8 - *"Finally, brothers, whatever is true, whatever is noble, whatever is right, whatever is pure, whatever is lovely, whatever is admirable — if anything is excellent or praiseworthy, think about such things."*

B. Satan is the father of lies and wants our minds to be filled with lies because they destroy us emotionally and spiritually.

   1. John 8:44 – *"He was a murderer from the beginning, not holding to the truth, for there is not truth in him. When he lies, he speaks his native language, for he is a liar and the father of lies."*

   2. John 10:10 – *"The thief (Satan) comes only to kill, steal, and destroy; I (Christ) have come that they may have life, and have it to the fullest."*

C. God, who is truth, wants us to believe and practice the truth because it sets us free.

   1. Isaiah 45:19 – *"I, the Lord, speak the truth."*

   2. John 8:31-32 – *"To the Jews who had believed him, Jesus said, 'If you hold to my teaching, you are really my disciples. Then you will know the truth, and the truth will set you free.'"*

D. Marital intimacy is often destroyed by the unbiblical beliefs (lies) we bring into marriage. Couples must *"be transformed by the renewing of your mind"* in order to enjoy marital intimacy.

E. The T.R.U.T.H. Model is a helpful tool in identifying and defeating lies that may be hurting your marriage.

   1. "T" stands for "trigger event"

   2. "R" stands for "reckless thinking" (lies)

   3. "U" stands for "unhealthy reactions"

   4. "T" stands for "truth"

   5. "H" stands for "healthy reactions"

F. The "trigger event" (T) level of the model is where marital events, both small and large, occur. Examples include:

1. Your spouse leaves his/her dirty clothes all over the place.

2. Your spouse puts you down.

3. Your spouse is indifferent to your requests for help.

4. Your spouse reacts angrily when you share your opinion.

G. The "reckless thinking" (R) level of the model is where faulty beliefs, attitudes, and expectations "play" in our mind. Examples include:

1. "My spouse should meet all my needs."

2. "Our marital problems are all my spouse's fault."

3. "I shouldn't have any needs in my marriage."

4. "My spouse owes me for all I have done for him/her."

H. The "unhealthy reactions" (U) level of the model is where destructive emotions and behaviors occur. Examples include:

1. Emotions like bitterness, resentment, hatred.

2. Behaviors like yelling, hitting, isolating, pouting.

I. The "truth" (T) level of the model is where the truth about the person, the situation, ourselves, and God comes into play to help us see the situation properly. Examples include:

1. "God created me with needs, but my spouse can't possibly meet them all. I will trust God to meet my needs through my spouse to the degree that my spouse allows Him to. I can trust my spouse and my needs to God."

2. "My unhappiness is not my spouse's fault. I choose to feel and act like I do, and to blame my spouse for how I handle things is wrong."

3. "The problems we have in our marriage are, for the most part, mutually created. While one person may have started things or may be doing more to create problems than the other, it still takes two to tango."

4. "My spouse doesn't 'owe' me when I do things for him/her. What I do is to be offered with no strings attached, and to feel that my spouse owes me reveals that I am doing things out of a wrong motive."

J. The "healthy reactions" (H) level of the model is where mature, Christlike responses to our spouses show up. Examples include:

1. Pleasant emotions like peace, contentment, joy, patience, confidence: and painful emotions like appropriate hurt, anger, disappointment.

2. Behaviors like speaking the truth in love, speaking words that edify, holding each other to provide comfort, doing things that help them when they have specific needs.

K. Developing the mind of Christ in marriage is a process and requires great commitment over time. Practical activities a couple can do to renew their minds and achieve intimacy include:

1. Keep a T.R.U.T.H. journal where you take situations in your marriage and break them down into the different levels of the model.

    a. the kinds of trigger events that set you off

    b. the faulty "tapes" that these events are evaluated with

    c. the painful emotions and inappropriate actions that you end up with

    d. the truths that you have tried to use to help you handle the trigger events better

    e. whether or not your emotional and behavioral reactions were helped by the truth

2. Memorize and meditate on Scripture verses that counter the lies you tell yourself.

3. Monitor your tendency to blame your partner for how you feel/act, confess examples of doing so to him/her, and ask for forgiveness.

L. Recommended Resource – *Lies We Believe Workbook*

Using the Genogram as a Basis for Insight, Healing and Intimacy

When important needs were met by parents in childhood, we develop the expectation that we will receive the same in our marriage. For example, if our parents were affectionate and supportive, we may expect our partner to be affectionate and supportive in the same way. Or, we may go into marriage anticipating that some of the things we missed from our caregivers will be met by our spouse when we marry. For example, if our parents gave us little attention, we may expect our partner to make up for that deficit. The genogram will help you assess the relationships that were a part of your childhood emotional development. A genogram is a pictorial representation of the relationships in your family of origin. For this exercise you will describe the major caregivers and siblings from your childhood (birth - age 18).

1. The Genogram Provides Insight into Emotional Pain from Childhood.

    A. Draw symbols for each of the caregivers who played an important role in your life — squares representing males, circles representing females. Draw symbols that represent you and any brothers and sisters. Birth order is represented from left, oldest, to right, youngest.

    B. Think about the relationships between family members. Was the relationship close, distant, enmeshed, conflictive, estranged?

    C. Who met your need for attention, affection, empathy, approval? What thoughts and feelings do you have about this exercise?

2. The Genogram Provides Opportunity for Healing Emotional Pain from Childhood.

    A. Face the hurt, then receive comfort. Avoid denying, minimizing, or spiritualizing the emotional pain from childhood. For effective resolution of past unresolved pain, an individual must begin with the hurt. One cannot forgive something which he or she refuses to acknowledge.

    B. Understand the truth – as the offenders and the offense are seen in the light of God's truth.

    C. Forgive the offender – as the grace of the Father's forgiveness is shared with one another.

3. The Genogram Provides a Basis for Intimacy in Marriage.

   A. Meet your spouse's need for attention. Seek to enter into his/her world. Convey appropriate interest and support.

   B. Meet your spouse's need for affection. Communicate care and closeness through physical touch and loving words.

   C. Meet your spouse's need for empathy. When hurt is shared, respond with understanding, gentleness, and reassurance.

   D. Meet your spouse's need for approval. Think and speak highly of him/her both privately and publicly.

The Healing Power of Intimacy
A New Resource for Classes, Small Groups, and Counseling

I. What is *The Healing Power of Intimacy*? How does it differ from other *Intimate Life* resources?

    A. *The Healing Power Of Intimacy* (*HPI*) is an interactive study guide designed for small groups, but also appropriate for individuals, couples, classes, and counseling.

    B. Rather than focusing upon deepening intimacy and responding to pain in specific relationships or stages of life (Married couples, parent-child, singles, separated or divorced), *HPI* focuses on the common denominator for all people: dealing with pain.

II. What is *HPI* seeking to accomplish? What issues are addressed?

    A. Like other *IL* resources, key elements of the "Intimacy Message" are presented:

        1. Our need for intimacy with God and each other

        2. Biblical truth not only presented, but experienced

        3. God's concern not only for our fallenness, but our aloneness

        4. "Intimacy Needs" (such as attention, affection, appreciation, and comfort) as the catalyst for intimate relationships

    B. *HPI*'s special focus is how to biblically and effectively deal with emotional pain.

        1. Pain is an inevitable, unavoidable part of life.

        2. Certain responses to our pain may be unproductive, even destructive to us personally, as well as to our relationships.

        3. Jesus' way of responding to His own pain provides an example for us to follow:

            ◆ Jesus faced His pain, rather than seeking to escape it. He sought others to be with Him as He faced it, instead of being alone.

            ◆ He understood the truth about: those who hurt Him, Himself, and His Father.

            ◆ He forgave His offenders.

            ◆ He freely loved others, even His enemies.

        4. God's plan is for our pain to be comforted and healed through intimacy with Him and each other— dealing with our pain as Jesus did.

    C. Thus, *HPI* aims not only to teach these concepts, but also to provide:

        1. Opportunities to reflect upon the concepts.

        2. Structured learning activities to enable participants to directly

experience the concepts individually, as couples and/or "journeymates," in class, small group, and counseling contexts.

    D. Core topics and learning experiences include:

- Understanding what intimacy is and is not. Why we really need each other.

- Identifying our specific relational "intimacy" needs and why meeting these needs is so important.

- Determining what we may have missed from our childhood years and how our current relationships may be affected.

- Clarifying sources of adult pain which may also need to be healed.

- Understanding how we may tend to handle life's inevitable pain: Four unproductive responses to our pain.

- Dealing with hindrances to feeling our emotions.

- A biblical approach to healing emotional pain.

- Emotional response to emotional pain: The comforting power of intimacy.

- How to respond if we have contributed to someone else's pain.

- Structured opportunities to experience biblical truths, such as Matthew 5:4, Romans 12:15, James 5:16, Ephesians 4:31-32, I John 1:9, II Corinthians 7:10-11, Isaiah 53, I Corinthians 12:21-26, I Peter 4:10, and others.

III. Who could benefit from working through *HPI?*

    A. Anyone!

    B. Prior exposure to Intimate Life principles and practices may be helpful.

- *HPI* would be an excellent resource to follow *Intimate Encounters, Parenting With Intimacy,* or *Discovering Intimacy.*

    C. Prior exposure to Intimate Life principles and practices is not necessary.

- *HPI* could serve as a beginning exposure to Intimate Life principles,

- It may be very helpful for those who especially need to address the effects of serious past hurt.

IV. How could you use the *HPI* pre-publication "field test" version?

    A. Take a free copy. You can photocopy it for use in your ministry.

    B. Use the "Feedback Forms" to tell us what was helpful or not helpful, suggest recommended changes, additions, deletions, different sequencing of content, suggest ways to improve ease of use, etc.

Intimate Life Classes

Introduction:

I. What Do We Mean By "Class?"

A class, in contrast with a small group, is a gathering of any size whose primary purpose is instruction. Key to Intimate Life materials and training for class usage is the emphasis on "experiential teaching"—participants actually experiencing biblical truths in the class! Classes may be elective, meaning that they have a specific number of sessions after which the class ends, or they may be ongoing, meaning that the class continues even after a particular course of study is completed. Either way, the size of the group is limited only by the interest level of the participants and the size of the room.

II. Why Provide *Intimate Life* Classes? Why Not Provide Small Groups Only?

A. There is no limit to the number of attendees (other than space).

Thus, larger numbers of people can be given the opportunity to experience the benefits of *Intimate Life* principles.

B. The "threat level" can be kept low.

The class setting provides the most comfortable environment for those who may be reluctant to address sensitive issues, or for those who may be new to a church environment.

C. Those who need and want further help often surface out of a class setting.

People often attend classes because their friends are present or because they are curious about a topic, rather than because they already know they need help with intimacy. As they are exposed to *Intimate Life* principles, many begin to realize that they desire and need what is being presented. Some of these couples then begin to ask for further help through small groups, mentoring, or counseling.

D. Discussion groups can be included, but are not required.

Some adults are willing to talk about personal matters, and some prefer not to. In a class setting, the teacher can choose to include a "discussion group" component. But effective classes can be conducted without them.

Note: One benefit of including discussion groups is that people who might not otherwise be willing to participate in a small group begin to get a positive "taste" of what *Intimate Life* small groups are like. Many eventually join a small group for more thorough work and accountability.

E. Visibility of regularly offered classes sends a strong message to the church: "Marriage, family, and friendships are a top priority!"

Whatever the church believes to be important will show through the classes which are offered. If knowing Bible doctrine or theology is most important, class offerings will reflect this value. If community service is the highest value, topics in classes will display this priority.

F. Classes can be conducted in neutral settings as community outreach.

Every conceivable setting has been used: hotel meeting rooms, apartment club rooms, schools, community centers, even a bridal shop!

G. Classes can provide additional adjunct help for those receiving counseling.

The counseling process can sometimes be accelerated. The counselee often benefits through seeing that many others have similar difficulties — they are not alone.

III. Are There Any Disadvantages?

A. Setting is usually less personal than a home.

Because of the size of the group, classes usually meet in church facilities or possibly other neutral sites (offices, hotel meeting rooms, apartment clubhouses, etc.) which may be more formal.

Yet for people who may not be sure they really want to delve into marriage issues and potential problems, these settings may be more comfortable than a small group meeting in a home.

B. Participants are typically less committed to doing the "homework."

Individuals, couples, even whole families desperately need to experience first-hand the truths of scripture applied to their relationships. These truths certainly include confession (I John 1:9), forgiveness (Ephesians 4:31-32), comfort (Matthew 5:4), praying for emotional healing (James 5:16).

People are more likely to experience these and other central "intimacy truths" if they do the "homework" for each session. Yet in a class setting, only 10 to 30% of the attenders actually do very much of the homework, because there is less accountability.

However, we should never assume that others who attend but don't do their homework don't benefit from simply coming to the class. Often class members are becoming more aware of what it means to have an intimate relationship, thus prompting them to seek further help through a small group or mentoring relationship. There can be great benefit to those who simply need the opportunity to more slowly "warm up" to these "intimacy principles" or to become more comfortable with the church at whatever level they feel appropriate. Also, experiential teaching involves class attendees in actually experiencing intimacy principles in the class.

THUS: Both classes and small groups are necessary for a comprehensive *Intimate Life* ministry in your church. People can then have regular opportunities to get involved.

IV. When Might Classes Be Offered?

A. Bible Study Times — ongoing or elective.

If ongoing classes exist, a particular class may wish to study these principles. But sometimes it is best to start an elective class specifically for the purpose of exploring and practicing these intimacy principles.

B. Non-Sunday Morning (as part of normal programming).

Many churches are offering Intimacy classes as a part of, or even in place of their normal Sunday Night programming for adults. Others are offering it as a part of their Wednesday night programming.

C. Non-Sunday Morning (as special outreach).

Some churches are offering Intimacy classes to their community at a neutral site with advertising, public endorsements, etc.

V. The Teacher of *Intimate Life* Concepts.

A. Who should teach?

The best teachers may not be the most articulate or glib people in the church. They may not be the most experienced teachers. But they are men and women who:

- ◆ desire deep experiences of intimacy in their significant relationships
- ◆ have directly experienced benefits and blessings of *Intimate Life* principles and practices.

  (See *Intimate Encounters* workbook, page 268, for other characteristics of effective teaching leaders.)

B. Who should not teach?

Occasionally people want to teach a class but don't want to be personally involved with the material. The goal is to help others, but not to experience the principles themselves. Because a core aspect of the *Intimate Life* message is that we must regularly and deeply experience biblical truth first-hand, and because *Intimate Life* materials provide multiple opportunities for these experiences in every class session, we believe that classes should not be taught by those who seem to want to avoid these experiences in their own lives.

VI. What Curriculum Is Available?

A. *Experiencing Marriage Intimacy* — based on *Intimate Encounters* workbook and *The Pursuit of Intimacy*.

This curriculum has 16 lessons, but could be adapted for shorter sequences. It includes suggested lesson plans, reproducible masters for handouts and transparencies.

B. *Parenting with Intimacy* and *A Design for Family Intimacy* – These interactive workbooks provide multiple lessons dealing with intimacy principles as applied to family realtionships.

C. *Intimate Family Moments* – Class material for pre-school, children, middle-school and teens—as well as parents.

D. *Discovering Intimacy* – For older teens, college and single adults.

E. *Restoring Intimacy* – How to save your marriage alone; material for those seeking to restore a broken relationship.

F. *Top 10 Intimacy Needs* – General intimacy principles for men, women, couples and singles.

VII. Scheduling Options for Intimacy Classes

The "Scheduling Options" handout suggests ways to cover the material in different time frames.

VIII. A Typical Lesson Plan

IX. Experiencing a Lesson

Intimate Life Small Groups

Introduction:

I. What Do We Mean By a "Group?"

    A. Roberta Hestenes, a leading teacher and developer of small group ministry, defines a small group as: ". . . an intentional, face-to-face gathering of 3 to 12 people on a regular time schedule with the common purpose of discovering and growing in the possibilities of the abundant life in Christ."[1]

    B. Why is 12 the suggested upper limit? Since most small groups meet for no longer than 2 hours and many for an hour to an hour and a half, even providing the time for as many as 12 people to say something during the course of the meeting may be a challenge. The opportunity to express oneself, to talk about what a person thinks and feels about something is precisely what a group offers that is not available in other settings such as large classes. When the group size increases above twelve, some participants will withdraw and become quiet, and the group will tend to depend on the instruction, insights, direction of the leader. Some groups will determine to limit their size to eight or ten in order to further enhance interaction from participants.

    Can two be a small group? Or are three required? Jesus said, *"Where two or three come together in my name, there am I with them."* (Matthew 18:20). The requirement for three could be met if two people were *"coming together in Jesus' name,"* seeking to improve the divine relationship of marriage, for example. As a couple asks for and receives divine wisdom to experience all that God desires for them as a couple, Jesus is an active participant in the group—there genuinely are three group members!

    C. What is the overall goal for *Intimate Life* small groups? Small groups have a specific purpose: discovering and growing in the possibilities of the abundant life in Christ. *Intimate Life* groups specifically emphasize the concept that abundant living is experienced through intimate relationships. Isolation, aloneness, loneliness are the enemies of abundant living. Thus *Intimate Life* groups for couples, families, children, teens and singles seek to:

- teach these *Intimate Life* concepts;
- provide practical exercises within the group sessions and as homework which help people learn not only what to do, but how to do it;
- help identify and reduce any hindrances to intimacy;
- provide positive experiences of intimacy principles and practices.

II. Why Provide Intimate Life Small Groups? Why Not Just Provide Larger Classes?

A. The key difference between a small group and a class, apart from the number of people present, is that participants in the small group are encouraged to commit to higher levels of participation. Key aspects of their commitment may include prioritizing group attendance and completing each session's homework prior to the next group meeting. This homework usually includes both individual assignments and a component of talking through the assignment with some-one else (a spouse for married couples as long as both partners are available, a friend or "journeymate" for singles). Thus much of the benefit of the group is derived from work *outside* the actual group meeting. Group sessions then involve members sharing their experiences of intimacy principles and practices and discussing key concepts from the material, with leaders modeling intimacy practices.

B. Moreover, the smaller number of people in an *Intimate Life* group provides more opportunity for the dynamics which have been found to encourage change:
- Opportunity to actually experience key biblical truths with another (or others) in the group
- Opportunity to ask questions, discuss, disagree and get a response to the expressed disagreement from several people
- Opportunity to witness change in others
- Opportunity to express emotion and receive comfort
- Opportunity to test new ideas and perspectives

C. In addition, a high level of emotional support and comfort can be provided to members who need to grieve major hurt. Consequently, small group participants typically enjoy significant fellowship, thus "experiencing God . . . through the church." People have often reported that these *Intimate Life* groups provided the first place they felt they could be honest and genuine about their own struggles.

III. Are There Any Disadvantages of Small Groups? Are There Times When *Intimate Life* Small Group Involvement May Not Be Appropriate?

A. The main disadvantage is that the small group process can be too threatening for some people.

B. This might be true for couples seeking to overcome the damage of adultery or other serious offense. A person or couple may be dealing with bitterness and anger which are too intense for most small groups. Someone may have experienced an intensity of pain which might overwhelm a group.

C. These disadvantages lead us to the need for churches to provide a special kind of help: couple-to-couple or person-to-person mentoring ministry. The content and process of the mentoring relationship is very similar to the small group, only with fewer people. Sensitive information can be protected and troubled couples or singles who need more intensive help can receive what they need.

The person or couple desiring to be mentored makes the same commitment that group members make. The mentor person or couple then leads them through the material in much the same way that someone would lead a small group.

D. There may also be times when we as group leaders feel that we may be "in over our heads." "When to Consider Referral to a Community Resource" is a guide designed to help you to evaluate whether or not a referral might be in order.

IV. Why is an Understanding of Small Group Dynamics Important for Group Leaders?

A. Small groups may vary in their purposes, levels of commitment, content, or type of leadership, but because of the number of people in the small group, participants tend to "behave" in certain definable ways. Participants in small groups tend to bring certain expectations to the group meeting, such as being allowed to express their opinions and feelings freely. These "small group dynamics" are different from how people tend to behave in larger groups of 13 or more. These dynamics also require certain behaviors from leaders in order for the experience to be positive for participants. At this point, we simply note that these dynamics do not arise from the particular personalities of group participants or leaders; rather, they are a function of the size of the group.

B. What if group members resist or are uncomfortable with their need to change? Because small groups are especially effective vehicles to invite people to evaluate their current patterns of living and to try out new ways of thinking, behaving, and dealing with feelings, some members of an *Intimate Life* group may experience tension which gets expressed in the group precisely because they are uncomfortable with the idea that they may need to change. If we understand that this tension is a predictable and often necessary aspect of change and growth, then rather than trying to squelch or ignore these expressions of tension or negative feelings, we will seek to draw them out, desiring to help the participant respond to them in a productive fashion.

V. What Types of Intimate Life Small Groups Could a Church Provide?

◆ Groups for married couples using the *Intimate Encounters* workbook.

◆ Groups for singles using the *Discovering Intimacy* workbook.

◆ Groups for parents and families using the *Parenting with Intimacy Workbook*, the *Intimate Family Moments Workbook* or *Design for Family Intimacy Study Guide*.

◆ Groups for those seeking to deal with marriage and family problems apart from their spouse using the *Restoring Intimacy* workbook.

◆ Groups for children or teens using the *Intimate Family Moments Workbook*.

◆ Groups for men, women, couples or singles utilizing the *Top 10 Intimacy Needs* materials.

VI. When Can Groups Be Offered? How Frequently Should They Meet? *Intimate Life* Groups Are Offered at Every Conceivable Time:

◆ During evenings in homes where participants enjoy a warm atmosphere and often more time for the meeting. These groups meet either every week or every other week. Some groups who are free to meet for 2 to 2 1/2 hours have found that the every other week frequency is adequate.

◆ On Sunday morning during the Bible study hour. These groups usually find that meeting every week is optimal.

◆ On Sunday evenings as part of the normal church program. In some churches, *Intimate Life* groups supplemented by occasional classes for the church or as community outreach have become the core of the Sunday Evening ministry.

◆ Some groups meet in the early morning or during the day.

The key is to determine what time and place is best for what the church is seeking to accomplish through these groups.

VII. What Type of Person Makes the Best Group Leader? Are There Certain People Who Shouldn't Lead an *Intimate Life* Group?

A. The best group leaders may not be the most articulate or glib people in the church. They may not be the most experienced small group leaders. But they probably are men and women who:

◆ desire deep experiences of intimacy in their significant relationships.

◆ have directly experienced benefits and blessings of *Intimate Life* principles and practices.

B. Occasionally someone wants to lead a group but doesn't want to be personally involved with the material. Their goal seems to be to help others, but not to experience the principles themselves. Because a core aspect of the *Intimate Life* message is that we must regularly and deeply experience biblical truth first-hand, and because *Intimate Life* materials provide multiple opportunities for these experiences in every chapter, we believe that groups should not be led by those who seem to want to avoid these experiences in their own lives.

Additional characteristics of effective *Intimate Life* group leaders are defined on page 269 of the *Intimate Encounters* workbook.

C. How can group leaders be trained? Most churches have found that the best training occurs through simply working through one of the *Intimate Life* group resources, especially in a small group setting. Thus, churches which regularly offer a variety of *Intimate Life* groups essentially have their own built-in leadership development program as a side benefit.

VIII. What Happens in a Typical Small Group Session?

See "Walking Through a Meeting," *Intimate Encounters* Workbook, page 270 for the basic components of a group session.

All Intimate Life Ministries materials contain suggestions for group use at the end of each chapter.

IX. Are There Different Scheduling Options for Using Intimate Life resources?

Yes! Each Intimate Life resource can be adapted for various schedules including 8, 10, or 13 week formats. Also, certain chapters can be expanded to provide the content for full weekend retreats.

X. Other Resources Available

A. Materials: Intimate Life Ministries study guides, such as *Top 10 Intimacy Needs, Heart Aflame, Spiritual Strongholds, Healing Power of Intimacy* and others.

B. Additional training opportunities are provided through Community Marriage Classes, Regional Conferences and Leadership Developmental Conferences.

XI. Experiencing a Group Session

1. Cited in Steve Sheeley, *Director's Workbook for Small Groups*. (Littleton, CO: Serendipity House, 1994), p. 19.

Intimate Life Counseling Ministry

Can churches actually provide an effective counseling ministry? And if so, what would that counseling ministry look like? How would a church get started? How would a church with an existing counseling ministry either expand its counseling or improve the effectiveness of the counseling being provided? This workshop will seek to answer these and other important questions. Particular examples will focus on a marriage counseling ministry with principles relevant to every aspect of counseling.

    I. Characteristics of an Effective Marriage Counseling Ministry in a Local Church.

        A. Ability to respond to crisis situation with immediate help.

            1. How does the typical couple "present" themselves for marriage counseling?

            2. What do they need from the counselor/counseling approach?

        B. Both "staff" and "lay" providers of marriage counseling.

            1. "Counseling economics," the challenge of "supply and demand."

            2. Factors which may increase the demand for marriage counseling:

                a. People begin to get practical help which really makes a difference.

                b. Your community begins to realize good help is available.

        C. Ability to address underlying issues as well as observable symptoms.

            1. Four stages of Intimacy Therapy

                a. *Assessment* – of individuals, marriage relationship, and intergenerational dynamics

                b. *Stabilization* – address factors **within** the couple relationship as a basis for improved functioning and additional therapeutic intervention

                c. *"Leaving/Cleaving"* – address **family of origin/ previous relationship** factors which contribute to marital discord

                d. *"Becoming One"* – encourage behaviors to increase intimacy, personal maturity, and positive mental health

2. The "Tip of the Iceberg" Challenge: Where does the counselor focus (particularly in stages 2 and 3)?

D. Commitment to work with the couple **together** whenever possible.

   1. Why might it be challenging to work with the couple together?

   2. Why is it crucial to work with them together?
A proposed goal for the counselor: Engage couple in process which helps them **experience** biblical truth together, especially:

    ◆ Confession

    ◆ Forgiveness

    ◆ Comfort

E. Transferability — couples who get help are involved in helping others.

II. How Mentoring Ministry Differs From Counseling Ministry

A. "Presenting" aspects of couple

B. Skill and/or experience of the provider

III. Suggestions for How to Begin or Expand Your Counseling Ministry

Marriage Intimacy Through the Life Cycle
Helping Couples from Newlywed to Empty Nest

A marriage relationship is a living, growing, organic entity, and it traverses through necessary and predictable growth cycles. Each of the five major marriage cycle phases (Courtship, Early Adult Life, First Mid-Life Transition, Second Mid-Life Transition, and Late Adult Life) presents a series of intimacy challenges. If these intimacy challenges are honestly acknowledged, confronted, and processed, each of the five phases offers a special opportunity for intimacy growth and intimacy enrichment. These five phases of the intimacy life cycle are epigenetic. That is, each sequential phase of the life cycle builds on the foundation of the previous phases. Efforts to deny or circumvent the intimacy challenges of early phases can severely distort the subsequent quest for ongoing intimacy in later phases of the life cycle. A couple's willingness to enthusiastically embrace the intimacy tasks of each of these marriage maturation stages insures that the couple can move progressively toward new plateaus of deeper intimacy and greater contentment across the entire life span of the marital union.

I. Phase One — Courtship
  A. Intimacy Challenges:
     1. Deferred resolution of differences ("I know he'll change once we're married.")
     2. Idealization of the partner ("She's perfect in every way. I know she will never disappoint me.")
     3. Blind attraction to a mate who is in rebellion against, or an imitation of, a parent figure ("I don't mind that you overcontrol me so tightly. This is better than a father who was never there for me.")
  B. Intimacy Opportunities:
     1. An opportunity to discover some of my own authentic identity as a separate person before merging with you.
     2. An opportunity to see beyond the illusion of who I imagine you are and to appreciate the reality of who you really are.

II. Phase Two — Early Adult Life
  A. Intimacy Challenges:
     1. Whose family are we going to recreate: yours or mine?
     2. How are we going to resolve the inevitable battle for control?
     3. How do we apportion what is "yours," "mine," and "ours" in the marriage (including addressing the very complex issue of financial sharing and financial management)?

     4. How do we synthesize two distinct family legacies? ("In my family we always...")

     5. How do we maintain the primary focus on our marriage intimacy (as the cornerstone of the family) with the encroachment of children?

  B. Intimacy Opportunity: Successful resolution of these control and priority issues in early adult married life creates a series of positive patterns or templates that will serve as foundation pieces for the balance of the marriage life cycle.

III. Phase Three — First Mid-Life Transition

  A. Intimacy Challenge: Can I finish leaving home (saying the final emotional and spiritual goodbyes to the family of origin)?

  B. Intimacy Opportunity: I can finally surrender the need to turn to my spouse as a surrogate parent. I can surrender the illusion that any single human person has the power to "kiss the boo boos and make them all go away." I can surrender the quest for a perfect mate and accept the "imperfect" mate with whom God has blessed me.

IV. Phase Four — Second Mid-Life Transition

  A. Intimacy Challenge: Accept and make peace with my physical mortality, grieve the empty nest, and surrender the illusion that any human person, thing or institution can serve a God-like role in my life.

  B. Intimacy Opportunity: Experience new freedom from the false quest to find ultimate security on human terms and discover within this freedom new reasons and new ways to be together as intimate partners for the second half of the adult life journey.

V. Phase Five — Late Adult Life

  A. Intimacy Challenge: Begin to view life from a perspective of Christian spiritual transcendence by gaining a fuller appreciation of the finite limitations of all worldly promises of security and immortality.

  B. Intimacy Opportunity:

     1. Gain a greater appreciation than ever before of the value of our intangible marital love.

     2. Find a closer spiritual union with God than at any previous phase of the life cycle.

     3. Discover that as we are individually making quantum leaps of growth toward God, we are simultaneously being collectively pulled toward even closer marital union.

Restoring Intimacy

How to Save Your Marriage Alone
A Reconciliation Ministry for Troubled Marriages

In troubled marriages, partners try to change or referee symptoms which often become the focus of marital conflict. A sense of hopelessness often brings couples to a point of separation. Understanding the concept of "emotional capacity" can aid in the restoration of a broken relationship.

1. You can only hold so much emotion before some of it spills out. A "cup" filled with unhealthy emotions will cause symptoms of stress and prevent positive emotions. Therefore, you need to identify what is filling your emotional cup, as well as your partner's.

2. Your emotional cup gets filled when needs go unmet. Comforting the pain of unmet needs is essential to freedom. Understanding the basis of your partner's unproductive behavior is essential.

3. Your emotional cup needs to be filled with comfort through emotional responding. It is important to identify what your partner might be feeling and consider how you might respond in a caring, supportive way.

4. Empty the anger from your emotional cup through forgiveness. It is critical to understand truths about forgiveness as well as hindrances to it.

5. Remove guilt from your emotional cup through confession. Accept responsibility for your part in hurting your partner. Show empathy toward your partner for the pain you caused. Agree with God that it is wrong to hurt your partner. It may be necessary to write a letter of confession to your partner.

6. Fears can be displaced from your emotional cup. Expect God to work in your partner. Be open with your partner about your needs. Focus on giving to his/her needs.

7. Unresolved childhood issues can leave your cup full of unhealthy emotions. Identify unmet needs, unhealthy thinking patterns, unhealed hurts and unproductive behaviors related to your childhood issues. Discuss with your partner his/her childhood pain and offer comfort.

8. Pour positive emotions into your cup by meeting intimacy needs. Share important intimacy needs with your partner and focus on giving to what you think your partner needs.

Goal Setting Retreats for Couples
Without a Vision People Perish

In Proverbs 29:18, Solomon said, "Where there is no vision, the people will perish." God, in His wisdom knew that we needed His laws to give us direction in our lives. Often times, we let the events of the world and other people dictate how we utilize our time instead of ourselves and the Lord. Time is becoming more and more a precious commodity. God is very interested in how we use the time that He has given us. Does your marriage and family have goals? Does your marriage and family really know where it is going? There are incredible advantages to setting and reaching goals as a family.

Advantages to Goal Setting

1. Goal setting is a basis for marriage and family oneness.
    Amos 3:3 poses the question, "Can two walk together, unless they are agreed?" In Genesis 2, God shares that His vision for a marriage is "oneness." This is oneness in body, soul and spirit. Setting goals as a couple helps the husband and wife to experience intimacy in all three areas. Furthermore, you do not feel that you are alone in the personal goals that you set.

2. Goal setting is a reminder of important priorities.
    People at school, church, your business, your neighborhood, in sports activities and everywhere else are demanding of your time. It has been wisely stated that, "Good things are the worst enemies of the best things." Often times we say "yes" to requests that we regret to some degree later. However, if a couple and family are informed and unified on family goals, it is easier to say "no" within already established priorities.

3. Goal setting offers a framework for decision-making.
    Life consists of endless pressing decisions: where to invest your time, attention, effort and money. By setting goals, a family faced with a decision simply asks, "Will this choice further accomplish our family goals or hinder them?"

4. Goal setting provides a sense of accomplishment and security.
    Fears that accompany feelings of insecurity and a lack of accomplishment fade away as couples set goals together. Families believe and feel that their future is secure together because there is direction and hope.

5. Goal setting is an example and witness to others.
    The world is starving for role models of what a healthy marriage looks like. As other couples see that your family has priorities and

actual plans to fulfill them, they will want to follow your example and experience oneness themselves.

Goal Setting Retreat

Getting away from the demands of life and developing goals in a retreat setting is an eternal use of any couple's time! Listed below are some suggested areas of goal setting as well as some examples in each category.

Spiritual

◆ Share prayer requests three times a week and pray for one another.

◆ Read the book of Proverbs in a month, one chapter each day.

Marriage

◆ Have a weekly staff meeting.

◆ Express daily appreciation of one another.

Family

◆ Take each child on an individual date monthly or quarterly.

◆ Begin weekly family nights for fun and conversation.

◆ Maintain family prayers together at meals.

Household

◆ Install deadbolt locks on all exterior doors.

◆ Develop a landscape plan for the front yard.

Financial

◆ Read two books on Christian financial planning.

◆ Establish a family budget and tracking system.

Career/Domestic Responsibilities

◆ Don't bring work home.

◆ Attend a Time Management course.

Personal/Social

◆ Read six non-fiction books this year.

◆ Develop two new sets of couple friends.

Ministry

◆ Volunteer as Sunday School teacher or worker.

◆ Join the church choir, greeters ministry, etc.

Tips for a Great Retreat

1. Do not bring your kids!

2. Attend a marriage support group and work through *Intimate Encounters* before you go on the retreat. Discussing the above goals can stir up some old issues that have been ignored too long.

3. A two and one half day retreat is preferred over the one and one half day. Goal setting is rewarding but hard work. Breaks in between planning sessions for relaxation are important.

4. See *Intimate Encounters*, chapter 14 for a suggested schedule for the retreat.

Women's Ministry – Touching the Entire Family
Intimacy Principles that Bring Healing and Liberty

I. Bearing in mind that the woman sets the emotional mood of the home, God is desiring to use the woman in the home to bring about healing and liberty. I Peter 3:1-4 clearly demonstrates how the woman who is led by the Spirit of God can, without a word, bring about spiritual awakening to her household. This is a powerful truth. Notice that this is one place where God is speaking specifically to the woman instead of the man. Her life is a powerful witness in the home.

II. The Women's Ministry within the church is touching the lives of women today, teaching women to "hunger and thirst" after righteousness. Women need to be with other women for encouragement and fellowship and are therefore more likely to attend a weekly Bible Study. We have an opportunity in ministering to women today to equip them to better recognize the emotional hurts, understand the truth about these hurts, and to walk in forgiveness. Wouldn't it be sensible for the church to teach a woman how to walk as Christ did, not only for her sake, but for her entire household?

III. Truths to minister to women:
   A. Understand biblical submission – submission is not stuffing emotions or believing that to speak out is to be unsubmissive.
   B. Emotions are God-given – consider the humanness of Christ and His emotions. "He was moved with compassion." Help women to understand the significance and positive aspects of emotion. Emotions were given as a blessing not as a curse. Help identify emotions.
   C. Help women to recognize past hurts – this can be very challenging because we have "stuffed" for so long. Also, contentiousness seems to be "a woman thing" as God addresses this in many passages in Proverbs. This would be an example of the woman who doesn't stuff, but hurls. This is the woman who comes across as "mean spirited." Both the stuffer and hurler are struggling with unresolved anger.
   D. Understand truth – Much of what women are acting out in their homes is not based on truth but on lies. *"The truth sets us free"* (John 8:32).
   E. Forgive and walk in forgiveness – now that we recognize and face the hurt and understand truth, we can forgive because we have Christ's forgiveness (Ephesians 4:32). As we understand His grace of forgiveness in our lives, we will be able to give grace and forgiveness to others.

F. We need others to comfort us – when Jesus was going to the cross, He needed His disciples to be with Him, by His side. In John 10:22-42 we see the contrast of Jesus being in the presence of the "religious" leaders who attack Him and He escapes their grasp. Then He goes back across the Jordan to the place where people "come to Him" and "believe in Him." We too, need others who accept us and comfort us when we are hurting. In every church, there are women who are unequally yoked or single, and therefore, are unable to receive comfort from a spouse. A women's ministry can help meet their needs.

G. Now that we have been comforted, we can comfort others. Guard against the syndrome, "I am the only one who feels hurt." The disciples were exhausted from grief and fell asleep when Jesus needed them most. Sometimes, as we focus on our hurt, we fail to see the deeper hurt of others.

H. Practical ways to let others know: I care about you; I trust you; I need you; I love you. — If we can't apply these principles in our everyday lives, we have failed in our teaching.

I. *"And my God shall supply all your needs according to His riches in glory by Christ Jesus"* (Philippians 4:19). Look to God to meet needs directly through His riches or through another.

J. Intimacy with God is the crucial foundation in developing intimacy with a husband.

IV. Many churches have a women's ministry that is ongoing.

Example of how this worked in one church's women's ministry.

Format: Wednesday Mornings – Fall and Spring

  9:00 – 10:00 — two choices for Bible Studies

10:00 – 10:30 — break for food and fellowship

10:30 – 11:30 — choices again were given, and the Intimacy Principles were taught at this time under the title, "Family Matters." Most of the women attended this class, which was an indication to us that this is a significant need today. This was not just a teaching time, but opportunity was given for the women to report back on homework and ask questions that they had about the homework assigned the following week. We used the material from *Top 10 Intimacy Needs* and *Intimate Encounters*.

Each week a handout was given with instructions on how to do the worksheet and make applications.

Testimonies: some couples began communicating for the first time and began experiencing deeper levels of intimacy; several couples joined the church; several couples began attending a "marriage intimacy" class offered through the church.

Men's Ministry to Tender Warriors
Developing Humility and Gentleness in the "Stronger Sex"

The American culture is confused about what it means to be masculine. Years of effort to blur gender distinctions have lead to a demeaning of "masculine" characteristics. Stu Weber in his book Tender Warrior observes, "Few object to a man being a mentor or a friend, (but) . . . authority and strength seem to be questionable virtues in our day. But we miss them in this turbulent, rootless culture of ours." "Soft" men appear to be a more desirable alternative to the stereo-typical "macho," insensitive, self-sufficient male; yet research consistently shows that so-called feminized men are very unhappy and ineffective in dealing with life. What does it mean to be a man? How might we encourage healthy masculinity among men, especially within the church? Our model is Jesus: "I am gentle and humble in heart . . ." (Matthew 11:29). Our culture and especially our families need Christ-like men.

I. What does it mean to be a "Christ-like" man?

   A. Humility: recognizing our God-given "neediness" and practicing mutual giving and receiving from God and others to meet these needs.

      1. The essence of humility is recognizing that we are dependently needy:

         a. Physical needs

         b. Relational needs

      2. Humble neediness does not equal weakness, immaturity, "female-ness" or lack of spirituality! It equals human-ness!

      3. Humility is a necessary prerequisite to Christ-like initiative; taking the lead in giving to meet the needs of others.

      4. Humility enables a man to receive what others give, because he knows he cannot meet his own needs alone.

      5. The humility of Jesus:

         a. Needing His Father

         b. Needing His friends

   B. Gentleness: allowing ourselves to feel emotion – for others, ourselves, and even God.

      1. Why is this so important?

         a. Feeling emotion is the key to experiencing biblical truth.

         b. Being able to feel is central to all intimate relationships.

2. Even strong men feel gentle tenderness for others
   (I Thessalonians 2:7-8). Gentleness is not weakness!
3. The emotions of Jesus:
   a. Mark 3 :1-6
   b. Matthew 26:36-46
   c. Matthew 9:36
   d. John 11:33
   e. John 14:8-9

II. How can we help men become Christ-like? How do we help
    develop humility and gentleness – men who acknowledge needs and
    feel emotions?

   A. Model these qualities with vulnerable transparency:
      1. In day-to-day interactions
      2. In classes, small groups, mentoring, and counseling
   B. Encourage through experiential exercises:
      1. Eight Commonly Identified Intimacy Needs
         Ask: "How do we feel when these needs are not met?"
         Ask: "How well can we meet these needs for ourselves –
         with no one else involved?"
      2. Healing Family Emotional Hurts
         Add: "Alone, list ways I have been hurt by my spouse
         and our marriage."
         Goals relative to emotions: Feel pain of his own unmet
         needs, the pain of his own sin and how it hurt others,
         the guilt of his wrongdoing, gratitude for forgiveness of
         God and others, and joy of restored relationships.
      3. Developing Intimacy Skills: Emotional Responding
         Goals: Learn to avoid unproductive responses to other's
         emotional hurt; learn to give empathetic comfort in-
         stead.
      4. Counseling Assessment – Genogram
         Goals: Acknowledge unmet needs from childhood,
         express the pain of those unmet needs, and receive
         gentle comfort from others.
      5. Childhood Questionnaire
         Same as for Genogram

III. Suggested Resources – *Top 10 Intimacy Needs, Intimate Encounters*
     and *Parenting with Intimacy.*

Parenting with Intimacy
A Practical Guide to Building and Maintaining Great Family Relationships

Relationships must come first! Children and teenagers grow physically, emotionally, morally, and spiritually only when parents are committed to building and maintaining intimacy with their children. Parenting with intimacy means directing, teaching, and disciplining. But, more than that, parenting with intimacy means imparting yourself to your child as you enter into their world, meet their needs, and dream with them for the future. Intimacy between parents and children not only means parents knowing their children and meeting their children's needs, but it also means parents allowing themselves to be known by their children.

Parenting with intimacy involves blessing your children in the following ways:

1. Focus on Selflessly Caring for Yourself.

    A parent cannot give what he/she does not have. Recognize the importance of the roles of mothers and fathers. Care for yourself physically, emotionally, and spiritually. Heal past hurts and disappointments.

    Keep your marriage strong and viable. The most precious blessing you can give your children is your strong marriage. A strong marriage not only nurtures the children, but it frees the child to grow up.

    Keep your own self-esteem strong. Know who you are in Christ. Avoid perfectionism — Your worth is not based in what you do or how well you do it. Your worth is based in being a child of the Heavenly Father.

2. Focus on Your Child's Needs, Not Just Their Deeds.

    To focus on our children's deeds is, indeed, important, but never sufficient. We must focus on their needs:

    a. Time
        Quantity and quality of time are important. Busyness is the worst enemy here.

    b. Attention
        Choose to enter into your child's life — daily. God Himself set the example here when He chose to enter our world through His Son, Jesus Christ.

c. Affection

Bless your child with physical attention — touching, hugging, eye contact. Bless your children by meeting their need for affirmation. Affirm them regardless of their level of performance. Affirm your children by teaching them about their feelings — especially anger, fear, sadness, and guilt. Help them appropriately identify and express their feelings. Impart yourself to your children by comforting their hurts.

d. Security

Commit yourself to protecting your children from the dangers of a fallen culture — the desire for wealth, the lust for sensual pleasures, and the thirst for power. Teach God's ways, thank God for the blessings He has given you. Commit yourself to healthy discipline for your children. This provides security and safety for growing up. Avoid harsh or permissive discipline, both of which are self-serving for parents.

e. Identity

Meet your children's need for identity by making them feel like they belong in your family, that it's OK to be a kid in the family, and their identity is greater than just the child of their earthly parents—They are a loved child of the Heavenly Father.

3. Focus on Preparing Your Child for the Future

Be a journeymate with your children by preparing them for the future. Identify and live for them lives of highest moral character and integrity. What you say or don't say, do or don't do about biblical values has a profound effect on your child's future. Teach and practice the foundations of healthy self-esteem. Our worth is not based on what others say; it is not based on what we possess; it is not based on what we do or how well we do it. Our worth is based on who we are—created in God's image, fallen but not worthless—and whose we are— sacrificially loved by the Heavenly Father.

Teach your children that trusting in God is the key to perseverance in the tough times we all face in life.

Avoid parenting with cynicism or fear. Impart the hope that comes from trusting in God.

Intimate Family Moments

Intimacy is God's idea. Proverbs 3:32 and Genesis 2:18 clearly state our need to relate to our Creator and the people whom He has created: "God is intimate with the upright" and "It's not good for man to be alone." We all long to experience close, warm,—intimate—relationships. This longing is most intense in the midst of family relationships. Several Old Testament words are used descriptively of this longing for intimacy. Reviewing these passages will provide us with valuable insights into the necessary ingredients for creating "Intimate Family Moments."

An intimate family moment means: You know me. The book of Job refers to "intimate friends" (Job 19:14). This Hebrew word for "intimate" (transliterated – YADA) is from the root word "to know" and speaks of deep personal awareness and understanding. Knowing our children means going beyond the conversations about school lunches and science projects. To deeply know a child means we know *his/her* emotional needs. To really understand a child means to know what he or she is feeling and thinking. God declares children as His gifts. We need to unwrap each precious gift— study, admire and become aware of the special uniqueness of each child.

An intimate family moment means: I can know you. Proverbs tells us that God is "intimate with the upright" (Proverbs 3:32). This reference to "intimacy" is even more startling as the word (transliterated – SOD) speaks of God disclosing Himself. He made Himself known by sending His Son. As family members seeking to develop intimate relationships, we too must be willing to self-disclose. A parent's self-disclosure ministers to a child's sense of aloneness. It removes the fear that a child is alone on his/her arduous journey to grow up. Just as growing up follows a predictable developmental progression, so does parental selfdisclosure. A parent discloses himself to an infant through tactile/sensory stimulation. An infant needs a parent who communicates acceptance, care and joy. For the toddler, parents can share their approval, empathy, faith and protection. The gradeschooler needs to hear about his/her parents' dreams, times of decision-making, and experiences of delayed gratification. The adolescent is ready to hear about a parent's painful feelings, times of temptation and the ways he/she is different from both parents. Finally, the young adult needs a parent who is willing to enjoy common interests, share regrets, and express a need for mutual giving. Great hope is prompted by the disclosure of our humanity as children hear and see Christ within us.

An intimate family moment means: You care about me. The psalmist tells us that God is "intimately acquainted with all [his] ways" (Psalm 139:3). This final Old Testament word (transliterated – SAKAN) speaks of "beneficial or caring involvements." One of a parent's most awesome challenges is caring for and involving themselves in affirming the identity of their child. As children come to embrace their incalculable worth to the Heavenly Father, they find security in belonging as a joint-heir with Christ and experience the competency of life in the Spirit. As adults, they will be prepared and motivated to lead the servant's life God intends.

Special Challenges of Single Parents
Ministry Needs and Opportunities

Single parent families are not second-class families! In fact, God has a special place in His heart for single parent families. *"The Lord protects the strangers; He supports the fatherless and the widow"* (Psalm 146:9). The church is the ideal place for these special families to get their needs met; yet many single parent families are misunderstood and therefore feel uncomfortable in the church family. It is our opportunity — our challenge — to reach out to these families.

I. The needs and stresses of single parents create special opportunities.

    A. Loss of marriage partner and parenting partner

    B. Home stability changes

    C. Financial stresses

    D. Friend and relative changes

    E. Feeling "left out" in the church

    F. New levels of fatigue

II. The needs and stress of children in single parent families create special opportunities.

    A. Loss of their most treasured possession (parents' marriage)

    B. Change in the home

    C. Feelings of divided loyalties (being in the middle)

    D. Feelings of blame, guilt, anger

    E. Feeling "lost" at church

    F. Higher risks for difficult behavior

III. Solutions for Single Parent Families

    A. Establish stability and predictability in all areas

    B. Single parents must keep themselves strong!

       — Grieve the losses

       — Avoid bitterness

       — Set priorities

       — Maintain boundaries and identity

       — Ask for support

C. Maintain the kids
 — Help them grieve the loss
 — Help them grieve the ongoing losses
 — Don't try to build or destroy relationships that aren't yours
 — Keep boundaries clear
 — Provide other strong adult role models and relationships

D. Find joy in life now

IV. The church as a divinely created relationship has the opportunity to help heal and support emotional and spiritual growth in single parent families

A. Avoid labeling these families

B. Avoid avoiding these families

C. Avoid pitying these families

D. Avoid conflicting messages

E. Give the message of love, grace, mercy

F. Give practical assistance

G. Practice inclusion

H. Meet relational needs — "Adoption"

I. Listen, trust and serve

Design for Family Intimacy

Satan attacked the first family (Genesis 4) and continues to assault families in our society. In America, two-thirds of all children will spend part of their growing up years in a single parent home. Child abuse seems out of control and a recent national survey indicated that the typical American father spends only fourteen minutes a week with his children — and ten of those minutes are spent in discipline. This seminar will help you develop an eight week course to counter Satan's attack on the family.

1. In the first week we discuss the ingredient of affectionate caring which says "I care about you." Caring involves reassuring family members and showing fondness, concern and attentiveness. We use the "Emotional Responding Principles" and "Selecting the Right Family Strokes" exercise to reinforce this ingredient.

2. In the second week we discuss the hindrances to affectionate caring, i.e., anger, bitterness or resentment. For encouragement resolving anger, we ask family members to memorize Ephesians 4:31 and lead them to practice confession and forgiveness.

3. In the third week we discuss the ingredient of vulnerable communication which says "I trust you." Trusting is the aspect in a relationship that risks being open about one's feelings, needs and hurts. We ask family members to complete the "Thanks/Wish List" exercise. We also distribute a sheet of fifty character qualities to aid in identifying things for which family members can show appreciation for one another.

4. In week four we discuss the hindrance to vulnerable communication, i.e., fear. For help releasing fears, family members are asked to memorize I John 4:18. We also lead them through an exercise in vulnerable praying.

5. In week five we expose family members to the ingredient of joint accomplishment, which says "I need you." This area of closeness comes from enjoying specific activities together. It involves setting and completing family goals.

6. In week six we discuss the hindrance to joint accomplishment, i.e., self-sufficiency. For help overcoming self-sufficiency family members memorize Galatians 6:2. We also have them participate in the Trust/Fall exercise.

7. In week seven we discuss the ingredient of mutual giving, which says "I love you." This ingredient is characterized by family members who think more highly of each other than of themselves. The focus is on "entering into each other's world." Each family member completes the "Eight Needs" exercise.

8. In week eight we discuss the hindrances to mutual giving, i.e., selfishness. For help addressing selfishness, family members memorize Philippians 2:3. In this session, family members develop a plan for taking the initiative to give to each other's needs.

Discovering Intimacy

A Relationship Ministry for College Students and Single Adults

Using The Discovering Intimacy Workbook With Single Adults

I. Introductory comments about single adults:

1. Single adults are a fast-increasing segment of the population due to young adults delaying marriage, as well as the high divorce rate.

2. Single adults are a too-frequently neglected population in churches which tend to be heavily marriage and family oriented.

II. Brainstorming Exercise About Single Adults

1. What conclusions have you made about single adults?

2. What do you perceive the needs of single adults to be?

III. Common misconceptions and myths about single adults:

1. Many people perceive single adults to have unstable relationships.

2. Single adults are often viewed as being in a holding pattern and rootless, which leads to the perception that they are somewhat transient and undependable.

3. More married people may regard single adults as less burdened by life's demands and therefore more able to serve effectively in the church.

4. Frequently, married people and single adults view each other as fundamentally different, which promotes less interaction among the two groups and perpetuates the "different" mentality.

IV. Some truths about single adults:

1. Single adults are actually quite similar to married adults in most respects, particularly in terms of their needs.

2. Single adults' friendship relationships frequently serve as their major source of getting needs met, as well as providing for others' needs; therefore, these relationships often are under much greater demand than married persons' extra marriage friendship relationships.

3. While some single adults, as is the case with some married adults, may be in a holding pattern, many single adults are,

in fact, stable, responsible citizens and members of churches.

4. The lifestyle of a single adult may at times be less complicated, not being encumbered by the demands of a spouse and family; however, the single adult is solely responsible for *all* household and personal tasks, which are usually divided in a married couple. Thus, the single adult is frequently pressed for time in carrying out tasks that may not meet his/her intimacy needs.

5. Perhaps the most significant area of difference between married people and single adults is not the difference in needs, but rather how these needs are met.

V. Using the workbook with single adults

1. The *Discovering Intimacy* workbooks teach that all humans, single or married, were created with needs that must be met in the context of relationships.

2. The workbook is designed to be worked through in the context of a relationship or relationships, such as a close friend or serious dating partner or in a small group format.

VI. How might you use the *Discovering Intimacy* pre-publication "field test" version?

1. Take a free copy. You can photocopy it for use in your ministry.

2. Start a *Discovering Intimacy* small group study.

3. Use the "Feedback Forms" to tell us what was helpful or not helpful, suggest recommended changes, additions, deletions, different sequencing of content, suggest ways to improve ease of use, etc.

VII. Other resources for single adults – *Top 10 Intimacy Needs*

"Nearly-Newly" Wed Ministry
Preparing Couples for the Challenging First Few Years

A separate class for newly and nearly weds is very important. They really don't fit in the singles or in the young marrieds. They are not really "single" any longer when engaged, and usually don't have children like the young marrieds.

Here is the strategy used by an Intimate Life network church for organizing and implementing a ministry to "Nearly-Newly" Weds:

1. For approximately a month before the class began, we saved the public records information from the newspaper. These records contain couples obtaining marriage licenses. It gives their names, ages and addresses. The week before the class began, we sent a letter and a flier to all those who were in driving distance of our church. This was about 100 letters.

2. We worked closely with the singles' pastor at our church. We asked him to encourage engaged couples in the singles department to come to our class.

3. We asked our pastor to announce from the pulpit that our class was starting. He was very supportive and was very helpful in promoting the class.

4. We put fliers in the church paper and in the church bulletin, announcing the class.

5. We talked to directors and teachers in the two youngest married adult departments and asked for referrals of couples who had been married less than one year.

6. We made sure that the people who manage the visitor center on Sunday morning knew about our class and where it was located. We asked them to be aware that young couples that came to visit might be newly married.

7. We had a booth at a bridal fair which was held in a large mall close to our church. We passed out fliers and brochures and talked to a lot of young couples.

8. We prayed to the Lord and asked Him to send us some young couples.

Our program works like this:

1. For 26 weeks, we study a book called "I Take Thee To Be My Spouse." All 26 weeks deal with different marriage issues, from a biblical perspective.

2. We then have our pastor come to our class and teach a lesson, which includes his marriage testimony.

3. For the next 13 weeks, we study the *Intimate Encounters* workbook. This course is designed to teach the couples how to have an intimate relationship with their spouse.

4. After a couple has been through all 40 weeks of our class, we send them back to their normal Sunday school class, based on their ages. If someone starts in the middle, we just start them there and keep them until they have completed the entire course. After the 40 weeks have been completed, we start the whole course over.

5. We have a fellowship with the class, usually in our home, at least once a month. This is a very important part of the ministry, to get to know the couples and them to know each other.

6. We have an outreach leader couple that helps us visit, and also have the class divided into groups, with couples from the class assigned as group leaders.

Key issues that we teach to the couples are:

1. Marriage is ordained by God. God made woman as a helper for man. God said that it was not good for man to be alone. He also said that a man shall leave his father and mother and cleave to his wife, and they are to become one flesh.

2. Marriage is a covenant, not a contract.

3. We define and discuss love. We teach that although feelings are involved in love, true long-lasting love is not a feeling, but rather a commitment. It is an unconditional commitment to an imperfect person.

4. Communication is one of the keys to marriage.

5. We study Ephesians 5 in connection with the role of a husband and the role of a wife.

6. We discuss and study the biblical plan for a sexual relationship.

7. Marriages will face times of difficulties and hurts. We teach that the newly wed couples must be prepared for disappointments. God uses disappointments to teach us many things, including trusting Him and unity in marriage.

8. We spend three weeks on budgeting and finances.

9. Marriage is a commitment for life. The rule is one man, one woman for life. There are seven keys to making a marriage work. These include change, forgiveness, compromise, communication, commitment, acceptance and love.

10. Conflict is a fact of life. We teach couples how to deal with conflicts when they occur.

11. In the thirteen week study of *Intimate Encounters*, we teach the couples how to develop intimacy in their marriage.

Prepare

A Pre-marriage Counseling Tool 80% Reliable in Predicting Happy Marriages

Using Prepare/Enrich in Premarital and Marital Counseling

  I. Introduction

 II. Why do psychologists and other mental health professionals use tests and test results in working with people?

    A. Testing may provide a large amount of helpful information in a relatively short period of time that would otherwise only be provided over the course of several sessions.

    B. Testing may also provide some important predictive information about a particular person or couple, based on his/her responses to questions on a test when compared with thousands of others who have taken the same test.

III. What are important concepts to understand when learning about tests and testing?

    A. Validity – The extent to which a test actually measures what it was designed to measure.

    B. Reliability – The degree to which a test will consistently produce the same responses over repeated administrations to the same person, usually reported as a reliability coefficient, such as .37 or .81.

    C. Normal Curve – Also known as the bell-shaped curve. That all human characteristics, when plotted on a graph, will usually take the form of a bell-shaped curve with most people clustering in the middle of the curve and fewer people represented on either extreme end. Important in understanding percentiles and statistics.

    D. Percentile – A ranking of where one stands in relation to 99 others, not to be confused with percentage. If someone scores at the 86th percentile, that person has scored higher than 85 others, but lower than 14 others.

IV. Why were the Prepare/Prepare-MC and Enrich Inventories developed?

    A. They were designed to help counselors and clergy focus objectively on crucial issues in relationships. Each Inventory is intended to assess both strengths and weaknesses in the premarital and marital relationship.

V. What are some of the features of the PREPARE/ENRICH Inventories that make them particularly valuable for use in both clinical and pastoral settings?

   A. The inventories assess 14 areas of functioning in the relationship, including broad measurements of relationship satisfaction and expectations.

   B. The inventories are psychometrically sound and have excellent validity and reliability. In addition, all of the inventories were normed using a very large norm base and norms are updated frequently.

   C. The inventories provide both individual scores for males and females, as well as norms for couple scores.

   D. The results focus both on strengths and growth areas that may be useful in developing counseling strategies for the couple.

   E. Each inventory is intended to be used with a complete feedback process which provides couples with a comprehensive evaluation of their relationship.

VI. What are the areas which the PREPARE/ENRICH Inventories assess?

   A. Idealistic Distortion – a scale which adjusts for social desirability in responses.

   B. Realistic Expectations – assesses an individual's expectations concerning love, commitment and conflicts in the relationship.

   C. Marital Satisfaction – a broad, global measure of satisfaction by compiling results of ten major areas of the relationship.

   D. Personality Issues – evaluates each person's perception of and satisfaction with their partner's characteristics as manifested through behavior traits.

   E. Communication – measures each person's beliefs, feelings, and attitudes concerning the role of communication in their relationship.

   F. Conflict Resolution – assesses a person's feelings, attitudes and beliefs concerning the presence and resolution of relationship conflicts.

   G. Financial Management – evaluates attitudes and concerns about how financial issues are dealt with within the relationship.

H. Leisure Activities – evaluates each person's preferences for using discretionary time.

I. Sexual Relationship – measures a person's concerns and feelings about affection and the sexual relationship with one's partner.

J. Children and Parenting – evaluates attitudes and feelings about having and raising children.

K. Family and Friends – measures feelings and concerns about relationships with friends, relatives and in-laws.

L. Equalitarian Roles – evaluates beliefs, feelings and attitudes concerning marriage and family roles.

M. Religious Orientation – measures attitudes, feelings and concerns about religious beliefs and practices within the context of the relationship.

N. Family and Marital Adaptability – measures the ability of a couple to change and be flexible when necessary.

O. Family and Marital Cohesion – describes the level of emotional closeness experienced among family members and the degree to which they balance togetherness and separateness.

VII. How do I administer, score and interpret the results of the inventories?

A. Administration guidelines.

B. Scoring instructions for computer-scored versions.

C. Interpretation of results (see hand-out for example).

VIII. Questions and Answers and Concluding Remarks

CHAPTER SIX

Additional Material on the
Intimate Life Message

Old Testament Reflections on Intimacy

"God is intimate with the upright" (Proverbs 3:32). *"It is not good for man to be alone"* (Genesis 2:18).

It's a fact. We need to relate—to our Creator and to meaningful others. It's true, just as the Bible says, it's not good to be alone.

Human beings long to experience close, warm, "intimate" relationships. Several Old Testament words are descriptively used of this need for intimacy. Reviewing several of these passages provides valuable insights into this key aspect of human "longing" and motivation.

Intimacy means you know me.

"...my intimate friends have forgotten me." (Job 19:14) This Hebrew word (transliterated—YADA) is from the root word "to know" and speaks of deep personal awareness and understanding. Surely it is God who knew us first—from our mother's womb and it is God who knows us best—as we arise in the morning, go throughout the day and retire in the evening. It's this deep inner "knowing" of one's heart, thoughts, and intentions that goes well beyond the mere sharing of facts, ideas, and opinions.

This "knowing" of one's spouse gives marriage special meaning and separates it from other human relationships as the "two become one flesh."

"Knowing" our children is a key challenge of parenting. Parents have received *"gifts from the Lord"* (Psalm 127:3) and the challenge is to "unwrap" them as we enter into each child's world and truly know them. This "knowing" and "being known" defines true fellowship within the Body of Christ. We are truly known by our Creator and have the privilege of knowing Him. Because of our intimacy with God we can truly know others and be known by them.

Intimacy means you care about me.

"Thou art intimately acquainted with all my ways" (Psalm 139:3).

This particular Old Testament word (transliterated—SAKAN) speaks of "beneficial or caring involvement" as a good God seeks not to withhold any good thing. In many ways this aspect of intimacy speaks to the motivation behind the "knowing." Why is it that God puts a priority on "knowing" me? It's so He can express His very nature of loving care. Notice also the breadth of this caring involvement: in ALL my ways! He knows me—all the failures, faults, and short comings, and still cares! *"While I was yet a sinner, Christ died for me"* (Romans 5:8).

Beautifully portrayed in this use of the word intimacy is the liberating motivation for marriage and family life. Why is it that I seek to enter into my partner's or child's "world?" Why prioritize time for these relationships? Why give sacrificially to other's needs? It's because I care! It's not mere duty, obligation, or in order to manipulatively have my needs met. This selfless, giving motive however, is not "natural," but rather, supernatural.

"Freely you have received, therefore freely give" (Matthew 10:8). Having received abundantly of the heavenly Father's divine caring involvement, a grateful heart overflows in selfless giving. It's this moment by moment gratefulness — the awe and wonder that my Creator and my Savior are caringly involved in all my ways — that prompts and empowers my intimate caring toward others. It also prompts my openness and longing to truly and intimately know this One who would so love me.

Intimacy means I can know you.

"But He is intimate with the upright" (Proverb 3:32).

This reference to "intimacy" (transliterated—SOD) is even more startling as the word speaks of God disclosing Himself; the Creator revealing His "secret counsel" to us, the created. We find the ultimate revelation of this self-disclosure in Christ as, *"the Word becomes flesh and dwells among us."*

In His High Priestly prayer of John 17, Jesus speaks to the eternal significance of this intimate "knowing" when He boldly declares *"And this is eternal life, that they may KNOW thee, the only one true God and Jesus Christ whom Thou has sent"* (John 17:3).

The Psalmist declares this longing of the heart to intimately know God in Psalm 42:1, *"As the deer pants for the water brooks, so my soul pants for Thee, O God."* This intimate "knowing" became the passion of the Apostle Paul's life: *"I count everything else as loss for the surpassing value of knowing Christ Jesus my Lord"* (Philippians 3:8). The intimacy of knowing this One brings forth the chorus of praise and worship in Revelation 4 and 5. *"Worthy art Thou, our Lord and our God to receive glory, honor, and power"* (Revelation 4:11). *"Worthy is the Lamb that was slain"* (Revelation 5:12). When we intimately know and humbly worship God, we then manifest His love to others as the *"Love of Christ constrains us"* (II Corinthians 5:14) to love a spouse, children, and others. Intimate love becomes contagious!

The "One Anothers" of Scripture

The creed for the 60's was expressed in the lyrics of a popular song written by Simon and Garfunkle—"I am a rock, I am an island." The idea was: "Be self-sufficient, impregnable, self-confident—each man to his own."

It didn't work in that generation — the self-sufficient attitude of the 60's led to the morally corrupt and materialistic mentality of the 70's and 80's, and the early church knew it wouldn't work in theirs. The creed of the early church was quite different: "We are a body, we need each other, we have all things in common." We could call it the "one another" mentality of the early church.

A fundamental aspect of God's plan for His people, revealed through Scripture and modeled by the early church is: *we need each other*. God has constructed His body in such a way that we are to be found mutually giving to "one another" for our needs. Have you ever noticed how often the "one anothers" are mentioned in the New Testament?

> **"Greet one another"** – *26 times*
>
> **"Comfort one another"** – *6 times*
>
> **"Love one another"** – *16 times*
>
> **"Teach one another"** – *4 times*
>
> **"Admonish one another"** – *2 times*
>
> **"Serve one another"** – *4 times*
>
> **"Honor one another"** – *2 times*
>
> **"Be devoted to one another"** – *1 time*
>
> **"Bear one another's burdens"** – *2 times*
>
> **"Accept one another"** – *1 time*
>
> **"Forgive one another"** – *3 times*

To admit that we need each other is not a sign of weakness, it's a confirmation of our humanity; it's not indicative of spiritual immaturity, it's an integral aspect of how the body of Christ functions.

Often, when a member of a Christian single's group finally becomes honest enough to admit, "I'm lonely," we often give this insensitive response: "Just trust God, He's promised to meet all your needs according to His riches." While it's true that God is the source of all good things (James 1:17), it's also true that He has sovereignly designed to often channel His supply through His body. Even Paul's declaration, "My God will meet all your needs" (Philippians 4:19) was written in the context of the saints ministering to the saints, and was specifically addressed to the church at Philippi who had "shared in my troubles," and, "shared with me in the matter of giving and receiving" (v.14,15).

The truth is, we all have an itch in the middle of our back that we can't scratch ourselves (needs that we can't meet ourselves). But everyone else has the same problem, and the answer is—mutual back-scratching (mutual meeting of needs through thoughtful, deliberate giving). It's the "one another" factor in Scripture, and it's a delightful aspect of how Christ's church was made to function.

Fundamentals for Effective Intimate Life Ministry

Passages for Memorization

Ephesians 5:18-21 *And do not get drunk with wine, for that is dissipation, but be filled with the Spirit, speaking to one another in psalms and hymns and spiritual songs, singing and making melody with your heart to the Lord; always giving thanks for all things in the name of our Lord Jesus Christ to God, even the Father; and be subject to one another in the fear of Christ.*

Romans 15:7 *Wherefore, accept one another, just as Christ also accepted us to the glory of God.*

Ephesians 4:26 *Be angry, and yet do not sin; do not let the sun go down on your anger...*

II Corinthians 6:1 *And working together with Him, we also urge you not to receive the grace of God in vain.*

Ephesians 5:25-26 *Husbands, love your wives, just as Christ also loved the church and gave Himself up for her; that He might sanctify her, having cleansed her by the washing of water with the word.*

Ephesians 5:22 *Wives, be subject to your own husbands, as to the Lord.*

Amos 3:3 *Do two men walk together unless they have made an appointment?*

Romans 14:10 *But you, why do you judge your brother? Or you again, why do you regard your brother with contempt? For we shall all stand before the judgment seat of God.*

Proverbs 30:15a *The leech has two daughters, "Give, Give."*

Proverbs 27:17 *Iron sharpens iron, so one man sharpens another.*

Proverbs 14:12 *There is a way which seems right to a man, but its end is the way of death.*

Hebrews 11:1 *Now faith is the assurance of things hoped for, the conviction of things not seen.*

Ephesians 4:29 *Let no unwholesome word come out of your mouth, but only that which edifies, according to the need of the moment, that it would give grace to those who hear.*

A Tale of Two Kings: The Power of Confession

At first glance, it seems unfair. One king sins by partially obeying the command of the Lord. The rest of his life is marked with problems, he loses the anointing of God on his life, and he dies an ignominious death. Another king commits adultery and then arranges for the murder of the woman's husband. He lives a full and meaningful life, dies at a ripe old age, and receives the epitaph, "He was a man after God's own heart."

The two kings? Saul and David.

For his first official assignment as king of Israel, the Lord told Saul to completely destroy the Amalekites. Saul only partially obeyed in that he spared the life of the king of the Amalekites and he saved the best of the flocks. His sin? A lack of thoroughness in obedience.

David, at the height of his career, committed adultery with Bathsheba and subsequently arranged for Uriah's death. His sin? Adultery and murder.

The fact that both men sinned does not surprise us for the Bible says, *"For all have sinned"* (Romans 3:23). What shocks us is the seemingly unfair result of their sinful acts. It almost seems that God inadvertently "switched" punishments. Surely adultery and murder deserve a more severe judgment than partial obedience! But the issue is not sin—*the issue is confession.* The question is not, "Which king sinned the most or the worst?" The question is, "How did each king deal with his sin?"

The Importance of Confession

When Samuel confronted Saul with his sin, instead of "coming clean" he avoided true confession and tried many substitutions. In I Samuel 15 we read that Saul:

Denied his sin – *"The Lord bless you! I have carried out the Lord's instructions"* (v. 13).

Rationalized his sin – *"The soldiers took sheep and cattle from the plunder, the best of what was devoted to God, in order to sacrifice them to the Lord your God at Gilgal"* (v. 21).

Blamed others – *"The soldiers brought them from the Amalekites; they spared the best of the sheep and cattle"* (v. 15).

Gave excuses – *"I was afraid of the people and so I gave in to them"* (v. 24).

Offered a flippant confession – *"I have sinned. I violated the Lord's command and your instructions. I was afraid of the people and so I gave in to them"* (v. 24).

Confessed, but only to avoid embarrassment and further confrontation – *"I have sinned. But please honor me before the elders of my people and before Israel; come back with me, so that I may worship the Lord your God"* (v. 30).

David, when confronted with his sin, confessed. He even wrote a song in which he pours out his contrite heart. The lyrics are recorded in Psalm 51:

"Have mercy on me, O God, according to Your unfailing love; according to Your great compassion blot out my transgressions. Wash away all my iniquity and cleanse me from my sin. For I know my transgressions, and my sin is always before me. Against You, You only, have I sinned and done what is evil in your sight, so that You are proved right when You speak and justified when You judge. The sacrifices of God are a broken spirit; a broken and contrite heart, O God, You will not despise. Create in me a pure heart, O God, and renew a steadfast spirit within me."

The critical difference between Saul and David was not the extent of their sin or the degree of its heinousness—but how they chose to deal with their sin. David confessed, Saul did not.

The Imperative of Confession

Is confession that important? Evidently so.

Sin will always put a crimp in our relationship with God. Psalm 66:18 says, *"If I had cherished sin in my heart, the Lord would not have listened."*

And if we're reluctant to confess, not only will it adversely affect our relationship with God, it will damage our earthly relationships. When relationships are violated and not properly healed by genuine confession—hurt, anger, bitterness, guilt, and resentment take root and begin to poison our hearts and damage our friendships.

Hurts are inevitable. It's impossible for two "fallen" humans to live together without eventually hurting one another. Likewise, it's impossible for parents to be "perfect" all the time; eventually we're going to wrongfully offend our children. When it comes to human relationships, it's not a matter of if we're going to blow it, it's just a matter of when. Therefore the issue is—what are we going to do when we offend someone?

When was the last time you said to your spouse, "I was wrong, would you forgive me?"

When was the last time you said to your child, "I was wrong, would you forgive me?"

If you're thinking, "Well, I think that must have been back in the late 1980's," your relationships are in trouble. In healthy relationships, confession and forgiveness will probably be recent and recurring.

Psalm 28:13 says, *"He who conceals his sins does not prosper, but whoever confesses and renounces them finds mercy."* The cover up is costly (does not prosper), the correction is clear (confess and renounce), and the result is sure (finds mercy—always with God, sometimes with others).

The Ingredients of Confession

Most of us, if and when we finally do feel that we need to confess, usually dilute our confessions with the same "disclaimers" that Saul used. We often:

Rationalize our offense – "I know I screamed at you, but I was so upset!"

Blame others – "I know I should have been home earlier, but my boss made me work late."

Give excuses – "I know I'm a workaholic, but I do bring home a lot of bread."

Offer a flippant excuse – "OK, I offended you, I'm sorry, but I'm not perfect you know."

Confess, but only to avoid embarrassment and further confrontation – "I'm tired of arguing and we need to go or we'll be late to the party. I've offended you, you've offended me, let's just say we're sorry and forget it."

To offer a sincere confession:

Be specific in naming your sin. Which of these two statements is more effective?

"If I've offended you or hurt you in any way, I'm sorry."

"I've been very selfish and insensitive. That's wrong of me."

Experience godly sorrow. True repentance comes from a broken and contrite heart. Unless we're sorrowful about our sin, a genuine change in our behavior will not occur.

Use the words, "I'm wrong" instead of, "I'm sorry." To simply say, "I'm sorry" might only mean, "I'm sorry I got caught" or, "I'm sorry you're so sensitive" or, "I'm sorry we can't get along." Whereas to say, "I was wrong" is a true admission of guilt.

Don't offer excuses. Our natural tendency is to confess that we were wrong, then offer excuses ("The reason I did that was…"), or we try to spread out the blame "I was wrong, but I wouldn't have done it if you hadn't…"). Put a period after your confession, "I was wrong."

Ask, "Will you forgive me?" At this point the ball is in their court. Forgiveness is an act of the will; it is a choice, not primarily a feeling.

How long has it been since you confessed to God and others? Ask God to show you specific areas which need to be addressed and then properly deal with them. Then adopt a lifestyle in which you're eager and quick to settle misunderstandings and disputes.

Intimacy with God: A Prerequisite for Intimacy with Others

Consider these two important facts:

FACT #1 – You can't give to others what you don't possess yourself.

FACT #2 – There are certain "divine commodities" which have their origin in God alone; they are only available from Him.

When considered together, these thoughts produce an important truth: An intimate relationship with God is a prerequisite for intimate, healthy relationships with others.

Here's how it works: Many of the qualities that are vital in our relating to other people are only available from God. Therefore we can only minister them to others to the extent that we have received them from God. For instance, here are four of these "divine commodities:"

Love

"Let us love one another, for love comes from God" (I John 4:7).

Comfort

"The God of all comfort ... comforts us ... so we can comfort others" (II Corinthians 1:3).

Forgiveness

"Forgive each other, just as God in Christ forgave you" (Ephesians 4:32).

Acceptance

"Accept one another, just as Christ accepted you" (Romans 15:7).

It's hard to imagine having an intimate relationship with a spouse, child, or friend without giving them steady doses of love, comfort, forgiveness, and acceptance. And since these qualities are only available from God, we must be constantly receiving from God if we hope to continually give to others.

Let's take a closer look at forgiveness. The evidences of unforgiveness in our society are rampant—49,315 new lawsuits are filed every day in the United States—that's 18 million each year! And the effect of unforgiveness on our culture is devastating—in 1991, Americans spent over 1.2 billion dollars on tranquilizers and anti-depressant drugs.

Do you have a hard time forgiving others? Is it easy for you to "hold a grudge," or are you quick to forgive? Unforgiveness is a breeding ground for anger, resentment, vengeance, and other vices, and will adversely affect all our relationships.

If you have difficulty forgiving others, you've probably never meditated on the fact that God has freely forgiven you (and continues to do so) for all the vile offenses you've committed against His holiness. Or you may understand the fact of His forgiveness (head knowledge), but you've never received His forgiveness (which brings emotional healing). The full impact of God's forgiveness is experienced as gratefulness flows from our heart; as we realize that the Father has cleansed us from all unrighteousness (I John 1:9). Once again, if you've not received forgiveness, you can't give it to others.

The whole concept of giving what we've received is the essence of Matthew 10:8, "Freely you *have* received, freely give." As we spend intimate time with God in prayer and in His Word, He "supplies all our needs," and then He can involve us in meeting the needs of others.

Developing Intimacy with God

"As Jesus and His disciples were on their way, He came to a village where a woman named Martha opened her home to Him. She had a sister called Mary, who sat at the Lord's feet listening to what He said. But Martha was distracted by all the preparations that had to be made. She came to Him and asked, 'Lord, don't You care that my sister has left me to do the work by myself? Tell her to help me!'

'Martha, Martha,' the Lord answered, 'you are worried and upset about many things, but only one thing is needed. Mary has chosen what is better, and it will not be taken away from her'" (Luke 10:38-42).

Are you a Martha or a Mary? Do you consider serving God more important than sharing intimate moments with Him? In these five verses, the Bible conclusively teaches what our first priority should be. We're actually taught the same lesson twice—from two different perspectives. We'll see the actions of someone who truly loved the Lord but chose to be busy (Martha), contrasted with someone who also loved the Lord but realized the joy and importance of spending intimate moments with Him (Mary).

First, let's set the stage for this drama. Jesus is in His third and final year of ministry—the year of opposition; in six months, He will be crucified. It is autumn and He is on His way to Jerusalem when He stops at a small village on the eastern slope of the Mount of Olives—Bethany. He has come into the house of friends—an unfamiliar situation for Jesus, for although the *"foxes have holes and the birds of the air have nests, the Son of Man has no place to lay His head."*

As the story unfolds, we notice that:

1. **Intimacy with God is His first priority for us: "only one thing is needed."**

   Martha misunderstood what Jesus wanted; He didn't want food, He wanted fellowship. Intimacy is the most important aspect of any relationship; it is the mainspring, the keystone. Many important transactions can take place after intimate moments, but none can precede.

   Furthermore, times of intimacy produce the proper perspective, the right motivation, and the necessary strength for "serving."

2. **Intimacy with God is more important than work/serving: "Mary has chosen what is better."**

   Busyness/activity can be the enemy of intimacy. Jesus considers "serving Him" to be a distraction when it takes the place of intimacy. By using a comparative adjective, Jesus doesn't condemn serving, He just says it must be put in its proper place—intimacy first, serving second. Max Lucado says, "Don't just do something, stand there!"—and that's good advice. Be still and know that He is God.

3. **Intimacy with God is a choice that must be made: "Mary has chosen."**

It's important to notice that these two women were sisters; they shared the same religious heritage, home atmosphere, educational system, and parental influence—their "environment" was the same. If Mary and Martha were raised in different homes, we might argue that Martha was the way she was because her parents put her on a performance basis, never took her to the synagogue so she didn't develop a reverent spirit, and her siblings abused her—and that's why she was so "works" oriented. Whereas Mary probably grew up in a home where there was ample attention, affection and vulnerable communication, she had a godly rabbi, and wholesome friends—and that's why she gravitated toward being a worshipper.

But that wasn't the case at all—they were sisters. At some point Mary made a choice; she chose to spend intimate time with Jesus. You can drift into being a Martha, but you don't drift into being a Mary—you choose.

4. **Intimacy with God is the antidote for anxiety: "You are worried and upset about many things."**

Martha was a worrier; not just on this occasion, but all the time. It was her normal "mode of operation," for Jesus commented that she was upset and worried about many things. People who are disinclined to intimate relationships tend to be worriers; anxiety is a persistent problem.

Since this Bible passage compares and contrasts Mary and Martha, it could be argued that not only does a lack of intimacy contribute to anxiety, but intimacy is an antidote for anxiety. Martha was upset but Mary wasn't!

Peace, tranquillity, composure, confidence, security, faith—these traits are enjoyed by people who have intimacy with God and others.

These principles of intimacy cannot only be applied to our relationship with God, they are applicable to earthly relationships. Consider these facts: intimacy with your spouse, family, and friends should be your first priority; it's more important than "serving" them or providing for their practical needs; intimacy is a choice you must make; and intimate relationships will displace anxiety with peace.

Let's consider three more observations concerning intimacy with God:

1. **Jesus seeks those with whom He is intimate.**

   There are three times in Scripture where we get a good glimpse of Mary, and in each incident she worships Jesus. Mary has a worshipping heart, and there's something attractive about one who understands the dynamics of intimacy. We know God the Father seeks those with whom He is intimate for Jesus said so in John 4:23. But evidently Jesus also was, and is, drawn to those who understand His deep felt needs. In John chapter 11, Jesus is heading toward Bethany where His friend Lazarus has been buried. It is a tense, emotional situation and Jesus knows that He will soon engage in an unusual demonstration of power—the raising to life of a man who has been dead four days. In the midst of this fast-paced, high-strung environment Jesus "asked for" Mary (verse 28).

   It's not surprising that Jesus seeks Mary's company for we have the same tendency. When you're in a trying circumstance, or for that matter, when things are "at ease," who would you prefer to spend time with—those who don't know your heart, or those with whom you're intimate? Charles Stanley says, "God doesn't have favorites, but He does have intimates." And God delights to share in the fellowship of those with whom He is intimate.

2. **Six characteristics of a person who is deficient in intimacy.**

   In this Scripture passage, we're taught truths about intimacy from two different perspectives; we're taught what intimacy is by observing Mary, we're taught what intimacy is not by noticing Martha.

   Martha no doubt loves the Lord, but she lacks the level of closeness that Mary enjoys. Her deficiency in intimacy is manifest in at least six ways. First, Martha exhibits a complaining spirit for she said to Jesus, "Don't you care?" Second, she shows no reverence for authority, for although she calls Jesus "Lord," she rebukes Him and accuses Him of not caring. Third, an attitude of selfishness prompts Martha to say, "My sister has left me to do all the work myself," and fourth, she exhibits a demanding attitude when she says to Jesus, "Tell her to help me."

   A fifth characteristic of one who is lacking in intimacy is a concentration on things instead of relationships. Martha was more concerned with food, house-cleaning chores, deadlines, work loads, and preparations than she was with visiting with Jesus. Finally, a person who is deficient in intimacy will be subject to emotional highs and lows. One minute Martha is inviting Jesus into her home, moments later she is upset and rebukes the Lord. We see a similar swing of emotions in

John 11 (the story of Jesus raising Lazarus from the dead). One moment Martha says to Jesus, "I believe that you are the Christ, the Son of God, who was to come into the world," but seconds later, when Jesus asks for the stone to be rolled away from the grave, Martha says, "But, Lord, by this time there is a bad odor, for he has been there four days." Martha is on again, off again. Full of faith, and then faithless. Whereas intimacy is the antidote for anxiety, a lack of intimacy leads to emotional instability.

3. **Three things that would appear to develop intimacy with God—but will not.**

As this episode is played out, we notice that Martha did three things that would seem to develop intimacy, but by themselves, they do not. *First, Martha acknowledged Jesus.* She opened her home to Him and even called Him "Lord," but there's a significant difference between acknowledging who someone is and developing closeness. Jesus made this entirely clear when He said, *"Not everyone who says to Me, 'Lord, Lord,' will enter the kingdom of heaven"* (Matthew 7:21).

Second, Martha was engaged in activity for Jesus. She was busy, but her activity for Christ was actually a distraction from the main thing. Jesus spoke of the inadequacy of activity when he stated, *"Many will say to Me on that day, 'Lord, Lord, did we not prophesy in Your name, and in Your name drive out demons and perform many miracles?' Then I will tell them plainly, 'I never knew you. Away from me, you evildoers'"* (Matthew 7:22, 23).

Third, Martha also was asking from Jesus; she was engaged in conversation but it was the wrong type of communication. Her conversation centered around things of the house, not issues of the heart. She went to the right source for answers and asked some interesting questions, but she still lacked intimacy.

These observations concerning intimacy are not only applicable to our relationship with God, they speak to our human relationships. Just as Jesus seeks intimate relationships, we normally "seek out" intimate friends. This is part of God's plan for relationships within marriage, family, and the church in order that we might enjoy the rest and security of intimacy. Also, people who are deficient in intimacy are likely to exhibit: a complaining spirit, no reverence for authority, a selfish spirit, and a demanding attitude; they will concentrate on things instead of relationships, and be subject to emotional highs and lows. When we observe these symptoms in ourselves or others, rather than react to the symptoms, let's employ God's antidote—intimacy. Likewise, just acknowledging someone, being active with them, or being engaged in "surface" conversation will not ensure the development of intimacy. Intimacy requires affectionate caring, vulnerable communication, and mutual giving to heart-felt intimacy needs.

Martha has taught us the hindrances to intimacy. Now, let's take a closer look at Mary, and learn from her key ingredients that *will* develop intimacy.

1. **Three things that will develop intimacy with God.**

   As the story unfolds, we notice Mary is engaged in three things that promote intimacy with Jesus. *First, she is close to Jesus.* The three times we see Mary in Scripture, she's always close to Him. It's difficult to develop intimacy in a long-distance relationship. Regardless of whether we're 100 feet or 100 miles apart, if we're not physically close to someone, the relationship will suffer. How close is close? Martha was perhaps in the next room, within shouting distance, but Mary was close enough to touch Him. That's the closeness that intimacy demands.

   Mary also portrayed a contriteness of heart. Notice her posture; she was "seated at His feet." Pride and an attitude of superiority are enemies of intimacy, but humility and reverence are its friends. In this Bible passage we see two humble individuals relating to each other— Jesus, who *"humbled Himself...taking on the nature of a servant"* (Philippians 2:7,8) and Mary, who delights to bend her knees and bow low before the Lord.

   Mary also concentrates on communication, she was "listening to what He said." What were they talking about? Though the Bible doesn't say, we might assume that they were engaged in that wonderful type of conversation we call vulnerable communication. There are, of course, two different types of communication. One type centers on facts, news, and topics dealing with day-to-day living—we might call it surface conversation. The other—intimate, vulnerable communication—centers around issues of the heart: feelings, needs, hurts, dreams, fears, plans, failures, and disappointments. When Jesus first entered Martha's house, perhaps those present talked about the weather, the latest fishing report, even "kingdom issues" such as the disciples being sent out two by two to heal the sick and cast out demons. It was probably an upbeat conversation. But once things settled down—Martha to the kitchen, the disciples visiting with Lazarus—Mary positioned herself close to Jesus, and perhaps the conversation changed to deeper issues and topics. Perchance Jesus was able to share with Mary how hurt He was at being rejected by those in his hometown of Nazareth, or the pain He was feeling because the religious leaders were spreading rumors about Him, or the opposition that was mounting in Galilee and Judea. Perhaps He even shared with her about His impending death. We do know that

Jesus found in Mary a listening, caring heart.

When two humble hearts meet, get close enough to touch, and engage in vulnerable communication—intimacy happens!

2. **Intimacy is the enduring aspect of a relationship.**

When Martha began to complain and question Mary's behavior, Jesus not only defended Mary's actions, saying that it was better than what Martha was doing, but He also pronounced that what Mary was doing "would not be taken away from her." Meals will come and go, news from the financial markets will be of short term interest, but intimate times will last. Intimacy is an asset stored in the heart; therefore it is enduring—it will last forever.

3. **Intimacy is the only way to understand the deep felt needs of the one loved.**

For our final observation, we'll need to go to John 12:1-8, the account of Mary anointing Jesus with costly perfume. Jesus repeatedly told His disciples that He would soon go to Jerusalem— and die, and yet few of them seemed to grasp the gravity of His statement. The disciples were more interested in who would be first in the kingdom. But in the midst of a dinner meeting, Mary pours a vial of costly perfume on Jesus' body, anointing His body for burial. Her demonstration of extravagant love is criticized by the disciples but Jesus defends her.

Perhaps Mary was the only one in the house that day who truly understood Jesus' deepest needs. Because of her intimate encounters with the Savior she had the unspeakable honor of sharing the deep feelings of His heart. That's what intimacy provides—insight into the deep recesses of the hearts of those we love.

These "principles of intimacy" can be used to deepen human relationships as well as our relationship with God. Apply these truths to your relationship with your spouse, children, and close friends!

Needs: The Motivation for Intimacy

"My God will meet all your needs according to His glorious riches in Christ Jesus" (Philippians 4:19).

The obvious premise of this verse is that we all have needs. If we didn't have needs, why would God promise to meet them?

No one teaches children to need attention, affection, or approval; they instinctively reach out for these, and other needs. Even secular studies document a newborn's need for nurturing, touch, and affection (Montague, 1971). And we don't "grow out of our needs;" our needs are continuous. Maslow (1970), observed and identified a hierarchy of needs, beginning with fundamental needs (physiological) and progressing to more complex needs (love and intimacy).

We discover the "birth" of intimacy through man's "neediness" in Genesis chapter 2. God placed Adam in a perfect environment with abundant provision, but although Adam's physiological and safety needs were being met by his Creator, God pronounced, *"It is **not good** for man to be alone"* (Genesis 2:18). Evidently Adam had been created with certain needs which God intended to be met in the context of human relationships. Apparently God desired not only for Adam to be the recipient of His divine acceptance, affection and encouragement—but also for him to receive them from meaningful human relationships. God therefore established marriage (Genesis 2:24), the family (Genesis 4:1, Psalm 127:3), and the church (Matthew 16:16-19, I Corinthians 12:27) as divine relationships through which needs can be met.

It becomes obvious that there's nothing wrong with having needs. We may err in how we go about having our needs met (expecting from others rather than having confident faith in God's provision will bring disappointment; demanding and manipulating will bring pain; and having needs met as an end in itself will be selfish), but to admit we have needs is not a sign of weakness, it's an acknowledgment of our humanity and our "poverty" of spirit (Matthew 5:3). It's also essential to resist the extremes of being selfish on one hand, and self-reliant on the other, or to be self-condemning (feeling guilty that I even have needs).

In the Bible, God is portrayed as a good God who delights to give good gifts (James 1:17), and who demonstrated His commitment to meet our needs (Romans 5:8). As a sovereign God, free to act without the confinement of human wisdom, God may choose to meet our needs "directly" or through His three divine relationships: marriage, family, the church. For instance, the church is called upon to accept one another (Romans 15:7), comfort one another (II Corinthians 1:3-4), love one another (John 13:35), and forgive one another (Ephesians 4:31-32).

Interestingly, several secular researchers have addressed this connection between relatedness, intimacy, and human need. For example, Clinebell and Clinebell (1970) actually defined intimacy as "the degree of mutual need-satisfaction within relationships." Fairbairn (1952) and Winnicott (1988), in their work in object-relations theory describe the basic human motivation as "intimacy seeking."

Carefully conducted research can, at best, only observe and confirm the truth of God's Word: *"It's not good for man to be alone"* and, *"God is intimate with the upright"* (Genesis 2:18, Proverbs 3:32).

Understanding Personal Needs

"A new commandment I give to you, that you love **one another***, even as I have loved you, that you also love one another"* (John 13:34).

Scriptures are filled with these "one another" passages which focus on **giving** to another. Each contains an **admonition** to give, but also a **need** which others must have. A study of these one-another passages gives insight into God-created **needs** which we have opportunity to meet.

Gratefulness for God's abundant and gracious provision to me, prompts me to a stewardship of giving to the needs of others (Romans 5:17, I Peter 4:10).

A Recent Survey of Top 10 Needs

- ◆ Attention (care)
- ◆ Acceptance
- ◆ Appreciation
- ◆ Support
- ◆ Encouragement
- ◆ Affection
- ◆ Approval
- ◆ Security
- ◆ Comfort (empathy)
- ◆ Respect

Thirty Intimacy Needs

As each one has received . . . serve one another as good stewards of the manifold grace of God.

1. **ACCEPTANCE** – deliberate and ready reception with favorable positive response – Rom. 15:7

2. **ADMONITION** – constructive guidance in what to avoid . . . to warn – Rom. 15:14

3. **AFFECTION (Greet with a Kiss)** – to communicate care and closeness through physical touch – Rom. 16:16

4. **APPRECIATION (Praise)** – to communicate with words and feeling, personal gratefulness for another – I Cor. 11:2

5. **APPROVAL** – expressed commendation; to think and speak well of – Rom. 14:18

6. **ATTENTION (Care)** – to take thought of another and convey appropriate interest, support, etc.; to enter into another's "world" – I Cor. 12:25

7. **COMFORT (Empathy)** – to come alongside with word, feeling and touch; to give consolation with tenderness – I Thes. 4:18

8. **COMPASSION** – to suffer with and through another in trial/burden – Heb. 10:34

9. **CONFESSION** – open acknowledgment of wrongs committed based upon inner conviction – James 5:16

10. **DEFERENCE (Subject)** – to yield or defer oneself to another for their benefit – Eph. 5:21

11. **DEVOTION** – a firm and dependable foundation of committed care – Rom. 12:10

12. **DISCIPLINE** – to reprove and correct when boundaries are crossed and limits exceeded – Prov. 23:13, Rev. 3:19

13. **EDIFICATION (Build Up)** – to positively promote the growth and development of another – Rom. 14:19

14. **ENCOURAGEMENT** – to urge forward and positively persuade toward a goal – I Thes. 5:11, Heb. 10:24

15. **FORGIVENESS** – to cancel out or "release" wrongs committed and bestow instead unconditional favor – Eph. 4:32

16. **HARMONY** – an environment of pleasant acceptance and secure love – I Pet. 3:8

17. **HOSPITALITY** – open reception of another with a loving heart – I Pet. 4:9

18. **INTIMACY (Fellowship)** – deep sharing and communion with another as lives are shared in "common" – I John 1:7

19. **KINDNESS** – pleasant and gracious servanthood – Eph. 4:32

20. **LOVE** – seeking welfare of others and opportunity to "do good;" consistent with having first been loved by God and seeing His value of others, the characteristic Word of Christianity – John 13:34

21. **PRAYER** – to entreat God's attention and favor . . . upon another – James 5:16

22. **RESPECT (Honor)** – to value and regard highly; to convey great worth – Rom. 12:10

23. **SECURITY (Peace)** – confidence of "harmony" in relationship; free from harm – Mark 9:50

24. **SENSITIVE (Same Mind)** – seeking to understand and accept another without judging – Rom. 12:16

25. **SERVE** – giving up of one's self in caring ministry to another – Gal. 5:13

26. **SUPPORT (Bear Burdens)** – come alongside and gently help carry a load (problem, struggle) – Gal. 6:2

27. **SYMPATHY** – to identify with another "emotionally" – I Pet. 3:8

28. **TEACHING** – constructive and positive instruction in how to live – Col. 3:16

29. **TRAINING (Equip)** – journey with me to model God's way of facing life's issues – Luke 6:40

30. **UNDERSTANDING (Forbearance)** – patient endurance of another's humanness – Eph. 4:2, Col. 3:13

Intimacy Ingredients: Helps and Hindrances to Intimacy

Intimate relationships – they must be developed and protected.

Intimacy doesn't just "happen," it takes conscientious effort to develop close, meaningful relationships. And once intimacy is established, it must be protected. This twofold emphasis is seen in John 10:10, *"The thief comes only to steal and kill and destroy* (Satan wants to destroy the closeness we have with God and others); *I have come that they may have life, and have it to the full* (one of the ways we experience a meaningful life is through intimacy with God and others).

Intimacy can be developed through:

- ◆ *Affectionate Caring* – "I care about you."
- ◆ *Vulnerable Communication* – "I trust you."
- ◆ *Joint Accomplishment* – "I need you."
- ◆ *Mutual Giving* – "I love you."

Intimacy must be protected from:

- ◆ *Emotional bondage* (hinders affectionate caring)
- ◆ *Fear* (hinders vulnerable communication)
- ◆ *Self-sufficiency* (hinders joint accomplishment)
- ◆ *Selfishness* (hinders mutual giving).

Let's take a closer look at these common hindrances to intimacy.

Affectionate Caring Hindered by Emotional Bondage

"Get rid of all bitterness, rage and anger ... Become kind and compassionate to one another, forgiving each other, just as in Christ God forgave you" (Ephesians 4:31, 32).

It's difficult, if not impossible, to have a caring, loving spirit if you're filled with bitterness, guilt, rage and anger. And these emotions/sins will damage all of your relationships, not just the ones to which the anger is directed. For instance, if you're angry with your boss, that anger will not only affect that relationship but it will adversely affect your relationship with your spouse, children, and friends. Anger poisons the soul.

Ephesians 4 teaches us that we must "get rid of" these vices (turn loose of, put away, empty out of us). This is done through forgiveness. Past hurts, even those suffered in childhood, must be properly dealt with in order to gain emotional freedom. Then we'll be free to be "kind and compassionate," and be able to engage in affectionate caring.

Likewise, the guilt I feel over my un-Christlike actions can be resolved through proper confession (James 5:16).

Vulnerable Communication Hindered by Fear

"There is no fear in love, But perfect love drives out fear" (I John 4:18).

Various manifestations of fear will hinder vulnerable communication:

◆ If I fear your criticism or rejection, I'll hold back from sharing my feelings, hurts, or needs.

◆ If I fear my own inadequacy, I'll hesitate to take initiative and avoid emotionally challenging conversations.

◆ If I fear being hurt, disappointed, or used, I may seek to control all situations so as not to appear vulnerable or needy.

◆ If I question your sincerity, genuineness, or commitment, I may demand to have it "proven" before I can accept it.

As we begin to understand and experience the perfect love of God, our personal fears are eliminated and we're able to vulnerably relate to God. As we learn to apply His perfect love in human relationships, these relationships mature, trust develops, and vulnerability deepens.

Joint Accomplishment Hindered by Self-Sufficiency

"I am rich; I have acquired wealth and do not need a thing" (Revelation 3:17).

"Apart from Me you can do nothing" (John 15:5).

A "Maverick, Lone Ranger" mentality is damaging to every relationship. If I think I can make it on my own, why do I need you?

The truth is, we need each other! God created us to be mutually giving to each other. Practically speaking, no one person has all the gifts, talents, skills, and resources needed to get the job done.

Self-sufficiency often develops through prolonged periods of unmet needs and the associated hurt which drives a person to deny his/her needs or to turn to self-nurturing ways to meet them (eating, fantasizing, achievement, perfectionism and other forms of escape). Self-sufficiency is also re-enforced by the "stoic, macho, hero" mentality which is often encouraged in our society.

To the contrary, when we look to one another and say, "I need you; I can't do this without you," or "We did it together!"—intimacy deepens.

Mutual Giving Hindered by Selfishness

"Do nothing out of selfish ambition or vain conceit, but in humility consider others better than yourselves" (Philippians 2:3).

Unfortunately, we often get so obsessed with our own needs that we neglect giving to the needs of others and we begin to take to have our needs met. Many relationships can be characterized by a take/take mentality, but there's no satisfaction in taking to have our needs met (there's a big difference between "taking" a hug and being lovingly "given" one). A relationship characterized by taking will soon show signs of resentment, discouragement, and distance. A relationship characterized by mutual giving will be satisfying, abundant, and intimate.

Take a quick check of your "relational vital signs." Do you have unresolved emotional baggage, are you hindered by fear, are you self-sufficient or selfish? To whatever degree these hindrances have crept into your life, they will adversely affect your ability to closely relate to others. Discuss these issues with your spouse or close friend.

Intimacy Ingredients from the Upper Room

A Topical Study from John 13-17

Affectionate Caring: "I care about you."

"Cast all your anxiety on him because He cares for you" (I Peter 5:7).

Relevant Scripture Passages

◆ *"Then He poured water into the basin and began to wash the disciples' feet"* (John 13:5).

◆ *"I will come again and receive you to Myself"* (John 14:3).

◆ *"But the Helper, the Holy Spirit – He will teach you all things"* (John 14:26).

◆ *"Peace I leave with you, My peace I give to you"* (John 14:27).

◆ *"These things I have spoken that my joy may be in you and that your joy may be made full"* (John 15:11/John 17:13).

◆ *"Your sorrow will be turned to joy"* (John 16:20).

◆ *"Your heart will rejoice and no one takes your joy away"* (John 16:22).

Vulnerable Communication: "I trust you."

"Men ought to regard us as servants of Christ and as those entrusted with the secret things of God" (I Corinthians 4:2).

Relevant Scripture Passages

◆ *"I have called you friends for all things that I have heard from my Father I have made known to you"* (John 15:15).

◆ *"From now on you know my Father and have seen Him"* (John 14:7).

◆ *"I will love him and disclose myself to him"* (John 14:21).

◆ *"When He, the Spirit of truth comes, He will disclose to you what is to come"* (John 16:13).

◆ *"The words which thou gavest me I have given to them and they received them"* (John 17:8/John 17:14).

◆ *"And the Glory which thou hast given to me I have given to them"* (John 17:22).

Joint Accomplishment: "I need you."

"I am the vine, you are the branches, he who abides in me and I in him, he bears much fruit for apart from me you can do nothing" (John 15:5).

Relevant Scripture Passages

◆ *"You also ought to wash one another's feet, for I gave you an example"* (John 13:14).

◆ *"He who believes in me—greater works shall you do"* (John 14:12).

◆ *"I chose you—that you should go and bear fruit"* (John 15:16).

◆ *"And you will bear witness also because you have been with me"* (John 15:27).

◆ *"As thou has sent me into the world I also have sent them into the world"* (John 17:18).

◆ *"That they also may be in Us that the world may believe that Thou didst send Me"* (John 17:21).

Mutual Giving: "I love you."

"A new commandment I give to you that you love one another even as I have loved you" (John 13:34).

Relevant Scripture Passages

◆ *"Greater love has no one than this that one lay down his life for his friends"* (John 15:13).

◆ *"I will ask the Father and He will give you another helper"* (John 14:16).

◆ *"I will not leave you as orphans, I will come to you"* (John 14:18).

◆ *"Because I live, you shall live also"* (John 14:19).

◆ *"Just as the Father has loved me, I have also loved you, abide in my love"* (John 15:9).

◆ *"While I was with them I was keeping them—and I guarded them"* (John 17:12).

◆ *"I desire that they also whom thou hast given me be with me where I am"* (John 17:24).

◆ *"I do not ask in behalf of these alone, but for those also who believe in Me through their word"* (John 17:20).

Vulnerable Communication: Lessons from the Psalmist

Our lives are filled with conversations which just skim the surface. Though often necessary, surface type conversations can only produce surface type relationships. To develop intimacy in relationships we must engage in vulnerable communication; a type of sharing in which we discuss feelings, emotions, hurts, and dreams. Granted, vulnerability involves risk, but it's worth the risk to experience the joy of intimacy.

Unfortunately, superficial communication can even become the norm in our talks with God. We utter a few ecclesiastical clichés and well worn phrases heavenward—and call it prayer. God certainly hears these prayers but just like in human relationships, they only produce a shallow relationship with Him.

What does vulnerable communication sound like? In intimate conversations, what do you talk about?

The book of Psalms, which served as the songbook of Israel, is a great textbook on vulnerable communication. Throughout the 150 chapters, David and other writers expressed a wide range of emotions and feelings. They were honest enough to share how they were feeling during the bad times as well as the good times.

Listed below are some of the many intimate topics discussed in the Psalms, along with an example (when applicable) of how Jesus vulnerably shared similar thoughts. Also listed are some "modern day" examples.

Topic	Psalm	Jesus	Modern Example
Frustration	*"All my enemies whisper together against me; they imagine the worst for me"* (Psalm 41:7).	*"Don't you know me, Philip, even after I have been among you such a long time"* (John 14:9)?	"I've been trying to get out of debt for years, but I keep getting deeper in the red."
Ask for help	*"Deliver me from my enemies, O God; protect me from those who rise up against me"* (Psalm 59:1).	*"Stay here and keep watch with me"* (Matthew 26:38).	"I'm having a hard time getting up in the mornings, would you call me every morning?"

Topic	Psalm	Jesus	Modern Example
Fears	*"The terrors of death assail me. Fear and trembling have beset me"* (Psalm 55:4, 5).	(no quote from Jesus)	"My company is planning a major lay-off and I'm afraid I'm going to lose my job."
Hurts	*"All who see me mock me; they hurl insults, shaking their heads"* (Psalm 22:7).	*"I tell you the truth, one of you is going to betray me"* (John 13:21).	"My boss embarrassed me in front of the entire office staff."
Self-doubts	*"I am like a deaf man, who cannot hear, like a mute, who cannot open his mouth"* (Psalm 38:13).	(no quote from Jesus)	"I'm not sure if I can do a good job of teaching my Sunday School class."
Plans	*"One thing I ask of the Lord, this is what I seek: that I may dwell in the house of the Lord all the days of my life"* (Psalm 27:4).	*"And if I go and prepare a place for you, I will come back and take you to be with Me that you also may be where I am"* (John 14:3).	"My dream in life is to own my own business."
Faith in God	*"Our God is in heaven; He does whatever pleases Him"* (Psalm 115:3).	*"I know that His command leads to eternal life. So whatever I say is just what the Father has told Me to say"* (John 12:50).	"I know God is going to see me through this difficult time."

Topic	Psalm	Jesus	Modern Example
Feelings of joy	*"He put a new song in my mouth, a hymn of praise to our God"* (Psalm 40:3).	*"I have told you this so that My joy may be in you and that your joy may be complete"* (John 15:11).	"I feel so fulfilled in my relationship with you as my spouse."
Confession of sin	*"Against You, You only, have I sinned and done what is evil in Your sight"* (Psalm 51:4).	(no quote from Jesus)	"I've been very insensitive to you lately. Will you forgive me?"
Hope	*"Now I know that the Lord saves His anointed; He answers him from His holy heaven"* (Psalm 20:6).	*"And now, Father, glorify Me in Your presence with the glory I had with You before the world began"* (John 17:5).	"Someday I hope we can have a child."
Words of encouragement	*"May He give you the desire of your heart and make all your plans succeed"* (Psalm 20:4).	*"As the Father has loved me, so have I loved you"* (John 15:9).	"I want you to know how much I appreciate your diligence."
Needs	*"Be merciful to me, O Lord, for I am in distress"* (Psalm 31:9).	*"I am thirsty"* (John 19:28).	"I'm going through a hard time; can we talk?"
The Lord's dealings in our life	*"I sought the Lord and He answered me; He delivered me from all my fears"* (Psalm 34:4).	*"You will leave Me all alone. Yet I am not alone, for My Father is with Me"* (Psalm 16:32).	"Lately, the Lord has been teaching me about being hospitable."

Topic	Psalm	Jesus	Modern Example
Past hurts	*"By the rivers of Babylon we sat and wept when we remembered Zion"* (Psalm 137:1).	*"If the world hates you, keep in mind that it hated Me first"* (John 15:18).	"When I was a child, my dad never told me that he loved me."
Discouragement	*"I am counted among those who go down to the pit; I am like a man without strength"* (Psalm 88:4).	*"My God, My God, why hast Thou forsaken Me"* (Matthew 27:46).	"Sometimes I feel like I'm not getting anywhere in life."
Praise to God	*"I will exalt You, my God the King; I will praise Your name for ever and ever"* (Psalm 145:1).	*"Father, I have brought you glory on earth by completing the work you gave me to do"* (John 17:4).	"I want to thank the Lord for being so patient toward me."

Unhealthy Thinking Patterns

If you repeatedly drive a car down a dirt road, over the same area, you'll eventually develop "ruts" in the road. In like manner, if you continually think a certain way over an extended period of time, you'll develop "ruts" in your thinking process and responses. We all suffer from these "habit patterns" of the mind.

These thinking patterns can control our outlook on life much like a special camera lens will affect what a picture will look like. A photographer will use different lens to achieve unique affects. A telephoto lens produces a narrow focus, a wide-angle lens provides a larger perception. A gray tinted lens will block out certain rays and produce a distinct color in the picture. In like manner, most people have a particular "lens" on their minds, through which they view life.

For instance, some people view life through the lens of pessimism. Their initial response to all events and information is negative. If it's a beautiful day, they think, "It may be nice now, but it will probably rain tonight." If someone compliments them, they wonder if it was sincere or if it was manipulative. In any situation, if there's 90% good and 10% bad, they'll focus on the 10%.

Other people observe life through the lens of oppositionalism. Regardless of what is suggested, they want to do the opposite. If you suggest, "Let's eat Mexican food for lunch" they'll say, "No, let's eat Chinese." If you suggest going to California for vacation, they immediately vote for Florida. If you want to buy a 13 inch TV, they lobby for a 20 inch. Everything is challenged and few things are accomplished without an argument.

Of course, not all lens are bad. Some people are optimistic — their motto is, "If life gives you lemons, make lemonade." Others benefit from a confident trust in a sovereign God, which allows them to view life from an eternal, Godly perspective.

Listed below are six unhealthy thinking patterns. These are mental "ruts" which can inhibit our ability to "think straight."

Personalizing

"Life events are personal rejections and attacks."

Personalizing is a distorted thinking pattern in which a person over estimates the extent an event is related to him/her. "Personalizers" tend to be moody and easily hurt by so-called rejections. Filled with insecurities, they develop low self-esteem and may blame themselves for everything. Others often see them as fragile, overly sensitive, childish, even hysterical.

Frequently, "personalizers" felt rejected or neglected in childhood or came from highly critical home environments.

"Self-talk" might include: "It's my fault. She's out to get me. He did that to hurt me. I can't do anything right. No one cares for me. Nothing ever goes my way. Life isn't fair."

Magnifying

"Making mountains out of molehills."

Magnifying is a distorted thinking pattern in which a person takes life's events and exaggerates them until everything seems like a catastrophe. "Magnifiers" may be volatile with anger, unmerciful with self-condemnation, or full of self-pity. Others may consider them self-absorbed, preoccupied with their own crises, whiny, and overreacting.

Frequently, "magnifiers" were raised in an environment in which little things were blown out of proportion. Spilled milk merited a character attack; discipline was excessive and out of proportion to the offense; or one parent was preoccupied with loneliness, rejection, or fear, which caused them to see catastrophes in every situation.

"Magnifiers" often use words and phrases like: always, never, every, devastated, worst, ruined, terrible, horrible, awful, beyond repair, too late, everyone.

"Self-talk" might include: "Everything is ruined. I haven't done anything right all day. I'll never have any friends. I might as well give up. He's always like that."

Generalizing

"History always repeats itself."

Generalizing is using past events to predict the future. Generalizing can undermine your hope, cast doubts on your adequacy, and prevent you from trusting others or yourself; it is a self-defeating attitude. "Generalizers" suffer from anxiety, doubt, and fear because they hold on to past hurts, failures, and rejections, and use them as evidence for predicting a negative future. They figure, "Why try? The past will just repeat itself," so they often lack initiative and are usually pessimistic.

"Generalizers" were often exposed to this way of thinking in their home environment. They might have grown up with "labels" such as: dumb, fatso, stupid, weirdo, rebel, which may have contributed to their negative generalizing about the future.

"Self-talk" might include: "An embarrassing moment of failure in sports means I'll never be an athlete. A low grade means I'm not a good student. I'll never be able to lose weight. I can't ever keep a job. I can never count on you to help me. We'll never be happy."

Emotional Reasoning

"Interpreting feelings as fact."

Emotional reasoning is a distorted thinking pattern in which feelings are confused with facts; reality is seen through the perspective of skewed emotions. Often, truth is denied because it doesn't feel right, and feelings become the major determination of truth. While the logical sequence is to think, then feel; emotional reasoning reverses that process.

"Emotional reasoners" often suffered from deep emotional trauma in childhood, such as physical or sexual abuse. Because of damaged emotions they often grow up disillusioned and irrational.

"Self-talk" might include: "I just feel that ... I don't care what you say ... I'm suspicious of him because ... That doesn't make any sense to me. I don't feel loved."

Polarizing

"Everything is black or white."

Polarizing is a perfectionist thinking pattern that views life as all-or-nothing, good-or-bad, black-or-white. "Polarizers" hold to rigid rules for evaluating life and classify events on the basis of their impossible standards. They feel no satisfaction in modest performance or genuine effort, and there's little joy in success since it was expected all along.

"Polarizers" often come from legalistic, nit-picking, performance-oriented homes or homes where there were many insecurities and fears.

"Self-talk" might include: "If it's not done this way, it won't work. They must be all for me, or they're against me. If it rains today, the picnic will be ruined. My project was criticized, therefore I'm a failure. My kid didn't make straight A's, something's wrong. We're having troubles, the relationship is doomed to fail."

Minimizing

"It doesn't really matter."

Minimizing is a distorted thinking pattern in which any significant event is denied or discounted. "Minimizers" tend to verbalize few emotions and expect the same from others. Even during life's major events they often demonstrate little or no feeling. They deny that anything troubles them.

"Minimizers" often come from homes where personal needs were neglected or overlooked. Instead of facing pain, they simply "shut down" and act like nothing's wrong. They learn to deny their own needs, which causes them to lose touch with their feelings and they become self-reliant and self-sufficient. "Minimizers" often become impatient with those who do show emotions.

"Self-talk" might include: "It's no big deal. It'll go away. It happens to everyone. You'll get over it. It doesn't bother me. I can live without it. That's life."

A Comparison Of How These Six Thought Patterns Might Be Manifested

John Smith has worked at a Fortune 500 company for the past three years. He just received a notice that, due to a down-turn in the economy, the company will be laying off 400 employees, and he's one of them. If John's predominate thought process is one of the six distorted patterns, he may think:

Personalizing – "I knew my boss didn't like me. When the decision was made about who to cut, he submitted my name."

Magnifying – "This is the worst thing that could possibly happen. It will probably ruin my life."

Generalizing – "I knew it was bound to happen, big companies don't care anything about their employees. This seems to always happen to me, I'll never be able to keep a steady job."

Emotional Reasoning – "I'm so angry, I could spit. Don't talk to me about 'economic conditions,' those lousy executives are just dumb."

Polarizing – "So that's the decision, lay-off's. If they don't want me, I don't want them. This company's going down the tubes."

Minimizing – "No big deal; no need to even talk about it. What's done is done."

During your next Marriage Staff Meeting, discuss to what extent you see these six thinking patterns in your life and your spouse's life. How were these "habits" formed? How have they affected your relationships? How can these patterns be overcome or eliminated? Together, study II Corinthians 10:3-5 and Romans 12:1-2 and pray together and ask God to free your mind from unhealthy thinking. Help one another "take thoughts captive" by offering truthful thinking when you notice your partner struggling with a harmful thinking pattern.

Developing an Emotional Vocabulary

Valentine's Day traditionally renews our attention, even for a brief time, to the remembrances of important relationships and the positive emotions they bring. In fact it's "good" feelings such as love and joy that tend to give life it's meaning. Without emotion, life seems to become a mere existence but with it, life takes on the potential of becoming *"exceedingly abundant, beyond what you can ask or think"* (Ephesians 3:20).

A. God is Emotional

Scripture is filled with references to God expressing emotions such as joy, compassion, grief and anger (John 15:11, Nehemiah 9:17, Ephesians 4:30). Certainly to be created in the image of God involves the capacity for us to experience and express emotion (Genesis 1:26). In a similar way, to experience and express LOVE from the myriad of potential emotions must somehow set human-kind especially apart since the Bible further reminds us that *"God is Love"* (I John 4:8).

B. Relationships Need Emotions

Deep and intimate relationships must include an emotional element. Many couples find themselves missing this emotional closeness even after years of marriage. Likewise children often go "under-nourished" emotionally as emphasis is placed on achievement, performance and other such "externals."

Of particular significance to emotional closeness is to develop a "vocabulary" of what one feels. Next comes open and supporting relationships in which feelings can be expressed and then reassurance and support given.

C. "Feeling" Project

During a class or group meeting, use some poster board to begin a "feeling chart." Divide the poster board into two columns for "Positive" and "Negative" feelings. Take turns naming as many feelings as you can (even 4 or 5 year olds can participate with "happy," "sad," "mad," etc.). See if you can name 15 - 20 positive and 15 - 20 negative feelings.

It's important to note that "negative" doesn't mean "wrong." It's how we handle our own negative emotions like anger or hurt that will be especially important. After a few times of developing a feeling "vocabulary" by naming feelings, you're ready to move on to sharing feelings.

How Do You Feel?	
Positive	*Negative*
Happy	Lonely
Loved	Sad
Excited	Afraid
Etc.	Etc.

Take turns sharing an event that happened during the day and then how it made you **feel**. You might start with each member sharing a positive event/feeling and then a negative event/feeling. This project can make a **major** contribution to developing a vocabulary of feelings plus validating that it's OK to feel! — and to talk about them!

Emotional Pain Over the Life Cycle

"In the world you will have tribulation" (John 16:33).

Prenatal/Birth Pain

Common Sources

- Maternal bitterness and resentment of pregnancy

- Emotional rejection of the developing fetus—unwanted, surrogate, etc.

- Attempted, but unsuccessful abortion

- Anger/conflict filled prenatal environment

- Problematic/traumatic delivery of the infant

Possible Outcomes

- Pain is totally emotional, pre-verbal, i.e., no thoughts associated with the emotional memory

- Emotional "flashbacks" of fear or rage might be expected

- Fearful, helpless, insecure, rageful

- Selected References: Lake, 1981; Rank, 1929

Childhood Pain

Common Sources

- Physical/Sexual Abuse – incest, sexual abuse, physical violence/beatings, etc.

- Emotional/Verbal Abuse – rage, ridicule, blame, enmeshment, criticism, etc.

- Passive Abuse – neglect, non-affectionate, non-empathetic

- Parental Divorce/Death/Adoption – abandonment, rejection

- Peer Ridicule/Rejection – cruel, humiliating remarks; embarrassing and traumatic "failure"

- Self-Inflicted (Narcissistic) – brought on by the unreasonable demands of childhood i.e., feeling displaced by the birth of a sibling; failure to be every teacher's "favorite" student, etc.

Possible Outcomes

- Common childhood symptoms of withdrawal, rage, depression, bedwetting, nightmares, etc.

- Many adult dysfunctions such as addictions, chronic low self-esteem, suicidal intentions, etc.

- Many adults continue to live out these childhood "scripts" i.e., you idiot, you're bad, you're worthless, you're to be used, you'll always be rejected, etc.

- Relationship difficulties through avoiding, "clinging," enabling, using, rejecting, etc.

- Selected References: Hemfelt, 1990; Conway, 1990

Adolescent Pain

Common Sources

- Parental Domination – over-bearing, intolerant home atmospheres prompt anger and undermine trust

- Parental Withdrawal/Neglect – "under-involved" parents wound a child's sense of worth and prompt fear of the real world

- Marital Discord/Dissolution – teens pay particular attention to adult relationships even though not admitting it; excessive conflict, unfaithfulness, separation and divorce produce intense pain

- Peer Rejection/Ridicule – romantic relationship break-ups, friendship betrayals and shame-producing traumas

- Self-Inflicted (Narcissistic) – idealism of unrealistic expectations inflicts pain

Possible Outcomes

- Moodiness, withdrawal and silence might be common among wounded adolescents

- Pressure for "belonging" (acceptance) is so great that some kind of accepting environment will be found

- Parents need to delicately balance "love" and "limits" carefully

- Listening more and lecturing less is crucial

- "Entering" into your adolescent's world to develop common interests is important

- Selected References: Carter, 1989; Lipsker, 1990

(Many of the childhood sources of pain and outcomes can obviously occur in the adolescent period.)

Adult Pain

Common Sources

- ◆ Marital Priorities – jobs, kids, parents, etc. are "felt" as more important than spouse

- ◆ Marital Unfaithfulness – through infidelity, disrespect, threats of divorce

- ◆ Marital Replication of Childhood Hurt – hoping to escape childhood pain only to have it repeated in marriage

- ◆ Child – disrespect, rejection, rebellion, humiliation

- ◆ Career, Friend, etc. – broken promises and dreams

Possible Outcomes

- ◆ Isolation replaces intimacy; manipulation and conflict replace mutual giving

- ◆ Blame and defensiveness common; seeking a more "ideal" spouse may follow

- ◆ It becomes essential to look "within" for the source of conflict and to God for the source of healing

- ◆ Healthy adults aren't satisfied with just "coping" to exist

- ◆ Selected References: Jagers, 1989; Backus, 1990

Healing Emotional Pain

God created us with three distinct parts—body, soul, and spirit (Genesis 2:7) and we can experience hurt and pain in all three areas. For instance, physically, we can suffer from: disease, broken bones, injuries, or natural atrophy. In our souls, we can suffer: hurt, grief, shame, fear, and rejection. Spiritually we can suffer: guilt, pride, and hopelessness.

There are many Scriptures which speak to the fact that God is our healer. Even one of His covenant names, Jehovah Rapha, means "the Lord who heals." One of the most critical areas in which we need the healing touch of Christ is in our emotions. Unfortunately, this dimension of healing is often neglected. We're usually taught a lot about transforming the mind, submitting our wills to the Lordship of Christ, having our spirits renewed, and our bodies healed, but seldom do we give adequate attention to our emotions. The Apostle Paul prayed for the Christians at Thessalonica to be "sanctified entirely, spirit, soul and body" (I Thessalonians 5:23) and an important part of our soul is our emotions.

Healing emotional pain is a threefold process. We must:

1. Face the Hurt

2. Understand the Truth

3. Forgive the Offender

All three steps are essential. Healing emotional pain is not simply "dismissing" the past; it's not a type of spiritual amnesia! Trite pronouncements like, "It's no big deal" simply don't work. Our emotions need to be "freed" to feel the hurt. Furthermore, our minds need to be renewed to embrace the truth about our hurt and our wills need to choose to forgive our offender.

The order of the three steps is important—We must begin by admitting our hurt; we can't forgive something we refuse to acknowledge. Furthermore, it's counterproductive to try to understand the hurt before we face it because then we'll be inclined to minimize the hurt or dismiss it, thinking, "that's just the way people are," or, "sure I got hurt, but not as bad as some other people." When we try to understand the truth of what happened before we face the hurt, we'll tend to minimize our hurt which will hinder healing.

Finally, after we acknowledge our hurt and understand the truth, then we are ready to exercise our will and forgive our offender.

Let's take a closer look at each area, even considering some examples from the life of Christ.

1. Face the Hurt

"My soul is overwhelmed with sorrow to the point of death" (Matthew 26:38).

The emphasis here is on emotions, not just the cognitive (mind) and volitional (will) aspects. How do you feel about what happened to you? Do you feel: sad, grieved, rejected, forsaken, ridiculed, neglected, despised, abandoned, taken advantage of, or unimportant? Avoid logical, mental responses, and don't minimize your feelings. Emotional expressions such as sadness, crying, and anger are to be expected and are even therapeutic. Allow yourself to grieve your hurt and loss. Share your hurt with someone who will empathize with you and comfort you. Then you'll experience the blessing of Matthew 5:4.

2. Understand the Truth

"For they know not what they do" (Luke 23:34).

When we experience hurt we often develop a distorted perception of ourselves, others, and God.

Misconceptions about ourselves – The trauma of personal pain often undermines our self-worth, which begins to build up defensive walls and makes us self-reliant. We may think, "I deserve to be treated badly" or, "If I'm open about the real me, I'll be rejected" or "I'll prove to you that I'm an OK person by gaining your approval, or being perfect."

Misconceptions about others – As a result of being hurt we may think, "No one can ever be trusted" or, "All men are evil" or, "My offender is a worthless villain."

Misconceptions about God – In response to our hurt and pain, we may think, "God can't be trusted" or, "He's too uninvolved to really care" or, "There must not be a God."

Understanding the truth in all these areas will produce freedom.

3. Forgive the offender

"Father forgive them" (Luke 23:34).

The focus here is on the will, not the emotions. We must choose to forgive our offender and do so on the basis that Christ has already forgiven us. Listed below are some of the common excuses given for not forgiving and a more appropriate, truthful perception.

Common Excuse	Accurate Perception
The offender hasn't asked for forgiveness.	Forgiveness is for my benefit, I shouldn't wait!
The offender hasn't changed.	What if God waited for me to change before forgiving me?
The offender doesn't "deserve" forgiveness.	Who does "deserve" forgiveness?
Punishment is appropriate . . . and I'm going to do it.	"Vengence is mine says the Lord."
It's my right to hold a grudge.	Holding grudges hurts me, not the offender.
I'll forgive after I feel like it.	Forgiving is primarily a choice, not a feeling.

The promise of Isaiah 53:5, *"By His wounds we are healed"* can be appropriated for our whole being—body, soul, and spirit! God wants to heal our damaged emotions and through the earnest application of scriptural principles, we can experience healing and freedom.

Dimensions of Marital Intimacy

For relationships to be knit closely together in marriage or in families, sharing must be encouraged. "Closeness" doesn't just automatically happen because we have the same last name or live under the same roof! "Becoming one" in marriage involves the freedom to share all of oneself—spirit, soul, and body.

The following chart illustrates how a husband and wife can develop marital intimacy in three dimensions. Marriages need nourishment and attention in each of these three areas. Just as we need air, food, and water to be healthy physically, our marriages have essential nourishment needs. A growing, healthy, and balanced marital relationship is one where each partner is enjoying the abundance of intimacy—spirit, soul, and body.

Often, couples may enjoy a certain level of spiritual compatibility, have a tolerable friendship, but have a problematic sex life. Other couples might enjoy a growing friendship and a satisfying sex life, but have no real spiritual closeness. Marital happiness is achieved when all three dimensions are constantly being nourished and experienced.

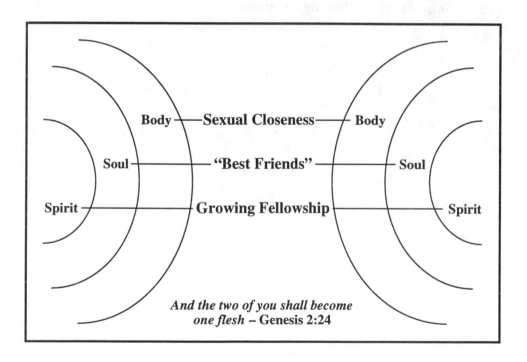

Body —— Sexual Closeness —— Body

Soul —— "Best Friends" —— Soul

Spirit —— Growing Fellowship —— Spirit

And the two of you shall become one flesh – Genesis 2:24

Spiritual Oneness

To achieve spiritual oneness, each partner must have a personal, vital, and growing relationship with Christ, and then learn to relate to his/her spouse on a spiritual basis. A good place to begin is to pray together. If either partner is uncomfortable praying aloud, simply hold hands and pray silently.

Another way to develop spiritual oneness is to begin a joint prayer list and share together in the blessing of intercession and answered prayer. Other ways to develop spiritual intimacy include: discuss selected Scriptures together; as a couple, begin ministering to others; and attend or teach a Bible study together.

Soulish Oneness

The soul realm involves the mind, will, and emotions. Closeness is developed as thoughts are shared and time is given in the loving act of attentive listening; emotions are identified and openly shared in a receptive and understanding environment; and a closeness of will is realized as common interests are shared, mutual goals are identified and achieved and oneness in decision-making is practiced.

Sexual Closeness

Physical closeness requires open communication, a priority time commitment, and the freshness of creativity. Plan a weekend away—without the children. Encourage sexual experimentation with new positions, locations, and sensual massage. Plan two sexual times together, just to focus on "giving" to your spouse, not taking.

Developing Spiritual Intimacy in Marriage

God created us with a body, soul, and spirit. We all have three parts, so when God declared that in marriage the "two should become one," He meant for us to become one in all three areas. Most couples find physical oneness (sex) relatively easy to "assess" or "count," soulish oneness a little more difficult to determine, but spiritual oneness—it's often too vague to even discuss.

For many couples, their individual spiritual life may be maturing, but their spiritual closeness as a couple is more a myth than reality. It's possible to have two people who are spiritual "giants," but who lack spiritual intimacy. These diagnostic questions may help assess your degree of spiritual oneness.

1. *Is your spouse supportive and encouraging of your personal spiritual growth?*

2. *Do you regularly practice the spiritual disciplines of confession and forgiveness?*

3. *Do you often talk about important issues concerning values and beliefs?*

4. *Do you ever pray together?*

Here are some suggestions on how to increase spiritual oneness in your marriage:

Commit yourself to personal spiritual growth.

In order to grow in spiritual oneness as a couple, each partner, as an individual, must be actively pursuing a close relationship with God. This personal nourishment will provide a spiritual focus for mutual sharing and will provide you with spiritual "goods" which can be shared with your partner. Personal spiritual growth can be enhanced by:

- Maintaining a daily devotional.

- Studying, memorizing, and meditating on the Bible.

- Participating in a small Bible study or discipleship group.

As a couple, participate in these spiritual "exercises."

- Discuss selected Scriptures together. During dinner, when you're riding in the car together, or anytime you have some free time—select a Bible verse and talk about it. For instance, relative to Matthew 6:33, *"But seek first His kingdom and His righteousness, and all these things will be given to you as well,"* ask each other these questions: What is "His kingdom?" How do we seek it? What are "these things?" Why does this verse begin with the word "but?"

◆ Pray together. If you have never prayed together, and feel awkward doing so, begin by simply praying silently together. Share some prayer concerns, hold hands, pray silently, and then squeeze hands when you're through. If and when you become comfortable praying silently together, try praying aloud. In addition to praying for others and for "things," be sure to pray for one another. It will bless your spouse and be a great encouragement to hear you praying for him/her relative to his/her fears, stresses, concerns, needs, and hopes.

Maintain two lists: a "prayer list"—where you record issues, people, and needs that you can pray for together; and a "journal of gratefulness"—where you can record answers to prayer, how God is guiding you as a couple, and thoughts of gratefulness and praise.

◆ Minister together. The key word here is together. For you to sing in the choir while your spouse teaches Sunday School is not together. It's not that you have to do everything together, but you should do something together as a couple. Lead a Bible study, work in children's church, sing in choir, participate in a mission trip, visit shut-ins—but do it together.

◆ Engage in various projects which will deepen spiritual awareness and involvement. Projects could include:

Read a book – select a Christian book that is of interest to both you and your partner, read it on your own, and then come together for discussion.

Attend a seminar – select a seminar to participate in and after attending, talk about what was presented.

Counsel someone in need – find a person or another couple that you can minister to and be available to counsel them, pray with them, or just "come alongside" them in their time of need.

Work on a "helps" project that is needs oriented – minister to some disadvantaged children, fix up a widow's house, take dinner to a family who's struggling, offer to baby-sit for a family who's dealing with a sickness or the hospitalization of a loved one, participate in a mission trip.

Spiritual oneness is often the most neglected aspect of a relationship but it is the dimension that offers the deepest sense of closeness and unity. Spiritual oneness provides a deep and enduring quality which transcends the physical and soulish aspects of a relationship. It is literally the "everlasting" aspect of a relationship, for though our bodies change and grow old, our spirits will last forever.

"Happy, Healthy Humans"
Key Developmental Issues from Birth through Adult

"Train a child in the way he should go..." (Proverbs 22:6).

Research consistently indicates that there are key developmental issues during all stages of life. Some parents erroneously think that developmental training need not begin until a child is 3 years old or older, but the admonition of Proverbs 22:6, *"Train up a child in the way he should go"* should begin the day a child is born.

A recent article in USA Today *(USA Today, Tuesday, April 12, 1994)* underscored the importance of early childhood development. Here are some of the comments from Julius Richmond, the first director of the Head Start program.

Why are the founders of Head Start, which has been aimed at 4-year-olds, now focusing on ages 0-3? The research on the development of the infant and young child is now so much richer and on a much sounder basis.

What have doctors learned about early brain development? We've learned that while the number of brain cells is fixed at birth, the way the nervous system essentially gets wired is not fixed and is very much influenced by the kinds of stimulation babies receive.

What factors affect brain development? Certainly, nutritional factors. But beyond nutrition, early stimulation has a lot to do with how infants and children come to relate to adults and other children, as well as their intellectual development.

What happens if the baby's environment is less than loving, if it is stressful? Any situation that overloads or interferes with optimal functioning of the brain would distort the way it functions. For example, a learning disorder associated with hyperactivity may develop.

A recent survey indicates that fathers in America, on the average, only spend 12 minutes per week with each of their children, and 7 out of 12 of those minutes are spent in discipline. From the child's perspective, this is a tragic statistic. A child, longing for attention, approval, and affirmation from one of the most significant persons in his/her life, instead, receives 7 minutes of discipline and 5 minutes of "who knows what" type of communication.

But the Bible teaches us to train a child in the way he should go, not just in the way he shouldn't go. This verse encourages a proactive position in raising children.

Beginning with infants and continuing through adulthood, here are some key developmental issues related to stages of life and some practical suggestions on how these issues can be positively reinforced.

Infancy

0 – 18 Months

Developmental Issues:

◆ Limited motor activity but very active senses...especially hearing, touch, sight.

◆ Judgments made as to the world being "safe" or "unsafe," especially in relationships.

◆ Judgments made are primarily related to whether basic needs for food, comfort, and nurture are met.

◆ Judgments are at an emotional level prior to verbal/cognitive processing.

◆ Judgments of caregivers are made as loving, comforting, caring, nurturing or rejecting, punitive, uncaring, and hurtful.

◆ Judgments made result in close emotional "bonding" (trust)...or emotional distancing (distrust).

Practical Suggestions:

◆ Provide visual stimulation and soothing talk and music.

◆ Nurture-nurture-nurture with touch, talk, and holding.

◆ Lovingly and consistently meet basic needs with gentleness and not anger.

◆ Express joy; smile and laugh around your infant; pray "over" child.

◆ Avoid raised voices, anger, over-protectiveness.

◆ Remove child from "problem" areas rather than discipline.

◆ Allow child to have a "favorite" toy, blanket, pillow, etc. as a security item.

◆ Begin to take short times away from the child—expecting crying; return with reassurance and comfort.

Early Childhood

18 Months – 3 Years

Developmental Issues:

◆ Rapid development of motor, verbal, and language skills.

◆ Autonomy needed in feeding and controlling elimination.

◆ Approval of parents and significant others is very important.

◆ Differentiating between acceptable/unacceptable behavior begins.

◆ Exploring/experimenting are essential to test limits and "survive" mistakes.

◆ Freedom to explore and receive positive re-enforcement says, "I'm OK."

◆ Freedom to make mistakes and yet receive acceptance says, "I'm OK."

◆ "I'm not OK," comes from over-protective, critical, demanding, permissive, neglectful, punitive environments.

Practical Suggestions:

◆ Stimulate motor development in walking, running, throwing, climbing, etc.

◆ Read-read-read to your child; Bible stories, nursery rhymes, and songs.

◆ Provide a safe environment in which to "explore" and express curiosity.

◆ Minimize "don't," "quit," "stop," "no," messages (though some are essential).

◆ Praise and encourage every "success;" pray "with" child.

◆ Teach-train-warn-discipline-reassure.

◆ "Distract" a child from "problem" areas rather than over-discipline.

◆ Discipline rebellion (but not childish acts) firmly, but gently...without anger.

Middle Childhood
Initiative vs. Guilt
3 – 5 Years

Developmental Issues

- ◆ Sense of competence comes out of freedom to undertake personally meaningful activities.

- ◆ Inquisitive, like to fantasize.

- ◆ Development of a functioning conscience.

- ◆ Desire to differentiate from others...my, mine.

- ◆ Initiative which is squelched by control or lack of opportunity produces guilt.

- ◆ Listening to child's questions and fantasies is important.

- ◆ Encouraging the freedom of choices is significant.

Practical Suggestions

- ◆ Encourage and praise "favorite" activities and interests the child enjoys; experience Bible songs, videos, and games.

- ◆ Talk about feelings as you see sadness, frustration, fear, rejection—develop a feeling "vocabulary."

- ◆ Encourage social interactions with other children—at home, church, pre-school.

- ◆ Give choices about clothes, play activities, snacks, etc.

- ◆ Apologize and request forgiveness for your temper, broken promises, etc.

Late Childhood

Industry vs. Inferiority

6 – 12 Years

Developmental Issues

- ◆ "Industry" is to set and attain personal goals.

- ◆ Social skills have heightened importance in rules, roles, sharing, and sexual differences.

- ◆ Capacity to reason develops and desire to be "useful."

- ◆ Sexual awareness grows and instruction needed.

- ◆ Acceptance from parents, peer group and other significant adults is important (teachers, coaches, etc.).

- ◆ Lack of acceptance/encouragement develops a sense of inadequacy/inferiority.

Practical Suggestions

- ◆ Find families with children the age of yours and initiate positive family friendships and positive peers.

- ◆ Explore and encourage hobbies, abilities, and talents.

- ◆ Identify and praise personal responsibility and unique character qualities.

- ◆ Have special "talks" and experiences to teach social skills such as manners, table games, social settings, etc.

- ◆ Continue affection from both parents, both verbal and physical.

- ◆ Begin open dialogue between mother/daughter, father/son, on sex roles and differences.

- ◆ Share feelings; heal hurts; teach biblical principles such as sovereignty, decision making, avoiding evil, etc.

- ◆ Communicate the Gospel clearly in word and life.

Adolescence

Identity vs. Role Confusion

13 – 18 Years

Developmental Issues

◆ "Explosion" everywhere...physical growth, increased mental capacities, feelings, and hormones.

◆ Body image, sexual identity, and social acceptance important.

◆ Independence, questioning everything and testing limits are expected, peer/parent conflicts common.

◆ Interpersonal relationship skills, psychosocial identity, and life direction help give "identity."

◆ Continual emphasis on competence goals in real life issues is important.

Practical Suggestions

◆ Look for hidden needs and fears underneath problematic behaviors; admit your failures and share your childhood struggles; apologize when you're wrong.

◆ Let natural consequences be a key discipline tool...i.e., give freedom to fail.

◆ Continue positive family friendships with positive peer influences.

◆ Ask "open-ended" questions such as, "Share something interesting about your day" instead of yes/no questions; affirm-affirm-affirm positive qualities, strengths, and decisions.

◆ Have special mother-daughter, father-son times such as trips, projects, goal setting, and Bible sharing focused on real life.

◆ Focus on big issues and don't nit-pick everything...you can't die on every hill!

◆ Don't panic when you hear "off the wall" ideas and comments. Teenagers love to say things for "shock" value.

◆ Continue to solidify spiritual growth through family devotions, ministry projects, and Christ-like example.

Young Adulthood
Intimacy vs. Isolation
19-30 Years

Developmental Issues

◆ Social relationships like courtship, marriage, and parenting are paramount.

◆ Experiencing intimacy with your spouse and friends is important.

◆ Career, social, civic direction needed.

◆ Intimacy development directly tied to identity issue...low identity, little intimacy.

◆ Without a healthy identity, young adults tend to move toward people in "clingy" dependencies, or move away from people by withdrawing into activity/self-reliance, or against people in hostility/rebellion.

Practical Suggestions

◆ Guidance becomes "suggestions" from a friend rather than "rules" from a parent.

◆ Discuss your parenting failures and regrets openly, seek forgiveness as necessary.

◆ Seek their input and advice in areas of their strength.

◆ Continue life training in real world issues such as finances, relationships, goals, biblical wisdom.

◆ Listen more, correct less; develop a few common interests.

◆ Dream together about the future.

◆ Accept friends and dating relationships, offer a safe environment and sounding-board.

◆ Continue family traditions at holidays and vacations, giving young adults freedom to participate.

◆ Reminisce often from positive family memories, special momentos, and your journal of gratefulness.

◆ As your young adult begins to "leave the nest," pray often for God's presence, direction, and blessing in decisions, relationships, and life directions.

My Childhood is Over
True or False?

Using the Genogram Exercise for Insight into Childhood

In one sense, we never "leave" our childhood. Childhood memories, sibling relationships, friends, parental influence, hometown environment — all leave an indelible impact on our lives and significantly impact who we are. Regarding these unchangeable events over which we often had little control, we must trust our past, our childhood, to our all-knowing, always-loving God and believe that He will cause *"all things to work together for good."*

On the other hand, God doesn't want us to continue to suffer from childhood hurts, fears, rejections, and losses; His desire is that we be free from past emotional pain. Gaining freedom from childhood hurts strongly relates to our ability to experience a happy marriage because an important part of God's plan for a healthy marriage is that *"a man should leave his father and mother and be united to his wife, and they will become one flesh"* (Genesis 2:24). The prescription is: leave, be united, become one, and the order of these three principles is important. You can't "become one" until you're "united" and unity isn't possible until you've "left" your childhood. As long as we're carrying emotional baggage from our childhood, "leaving" will be difficult if not impossible.

Perhaps the first step in gaining freedom from childhood hurts is to draw a genogram. A genogram is a pictorial representation of the relationships in your family, showing your major caregivers, siblings, and other individuals who played an important role in your life.

To develop your chart, begin by drawing symbols for each of the influential adults in your life (squares represent males and circles represent females). Next, draw symbols that represent you and any brothers and sisters (birth order is represented from left, oldest – to right, youngest). Finally, draw symbols for anyone else who significantly influenced your life (grandparents, aunts, uncles, special friends).

Using the signs listed in the Key, indicate the quality of the relationships. For instance, was the relationship close, with a lot of sharing and communication, or was the relationship distant, with little intimacy, emotional contact, or vulnerable communication? Was a relationship conflictive, with frequent arguments and hostility? Was the relationship estranged because of silence, rejection, abandonment, or punishment?

A genogram helps clarify childhood relationships and will reveal relationships in which potential hurt was developed — relationships that must be properly dealt with if "leaving and uniting" are to become a reality. Also, it will serve as a catalyst for appreciation for those relationships which were wholesome and fulfilling.

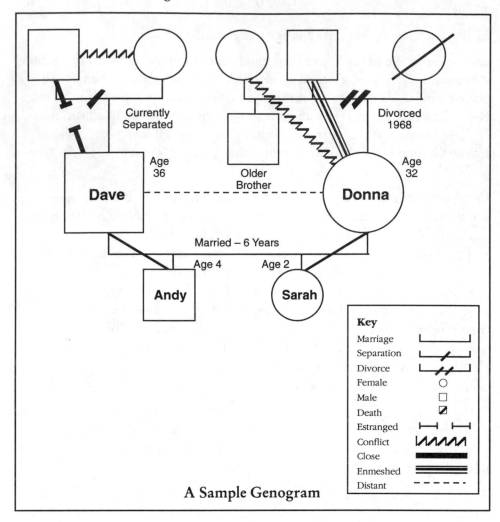

A Sample Genogram

Chapter eleven of *Intimate Encounters* teaches what to do with the genogram once it is developed. Pertinent questions will help you understand the dynamics of needs which were met or unmet and how your upbringing has shaped your personality. The genogram exercise can be one of the most liberating activities you'll ever engage in. The genogram exercise can also be completed as a family project, giving each family member an opportunity to characterize the quality of relationships from their perspective.

Don't Hurt Alone

"This is why I weep and my eyes overflow with tears. No one is near to comfort me, no one to restore my spirit" (Lamentations 1:16).

It was around 9:30 in the morning on Wednesday, October 14, 1987 when 18-month-old Jessica McClure slipped down the 8 inch pipe of an abandoned well shaft. When rescue workers arrived, Jessica was 22 feet below the ground, where she would be trapped for the next 58 hours.

The rescue strategy was simple: drill a parallel shaft next to the one where Jessica was trapped, then tunnel across and remove her. Within 10 hours the workers had drilled within 2 feet of the frightened and dehydrated child, but then all hopes for a quick rescue were dashed when the diggers hit a solid outcropping of limestone. The hard rock snapped expensive diamond-tipped drill bits and the tight quarters quickly exhausted the workers — 30 minutes was the maximum time that any of them could work in the shaft.

But finally the hard work and expertise of hundreds of workers and the prayers of a nation came to a triumphal ending when paramedics Robert O'Donnell and Steve Forbes wrapped Jessica on an immobilization board and headed for the surface. Jessica was fine.

How was an 18-month-old child able to survive a seemingly impossible ordeal? Jessica was hurting — but she wasn't hurting alone.

Perhaps the one thing that gave Jessica the strength and determination to persevere was the fact that the rescue workers immediately and continually communicated to her — they removed her "aloneness."

At the beginning of the tragic accident, a microphone was dropped into the hole to establish communication. Later, a video camera was used to establish visual contact. Rescue workers talked to her constantly. Detective Andy Glasscock reported that, "We began to shout down the well, and Jessica responded with whimpers and cries. After listening to her for so long, I could tell her moods. When we weren't calling words of encouragement, we'd tell her to sing for us. I'll never forget her singing 'Winnie the Pooh.' We'd say, 'How does a kitten go?' and she'd respond to us."

Bobbie Jo Hall, a police officer, stated that, "We took turns staying by the hole talking to her. Every time she'd cry or whimper, it was kind of a 'Help me, I'm hurt' kind of whimper. Sometimes she would go 30 or 40 minutes without a sound, and we'd get hysterical and start calling her again until we'd get a response."

Jessica was hurting — but she wasn't hurting alone.

Life is full of hurtful times. We may not be trapped inside an 8 inch pipe below the earth but we may be trapped in a black hole of depression from which there seems to be no way out. We may not be physically dehydrated, but we may be mentally and emotionally exhausted.

It always hurts to hurt — that's intrinsic; but to hurt alone is insufferable.

Why would anyone ever hurt alone? One possible answer would be — we don't have anyone who will hurt with us. That's why it's important, even necessary, to have a "journeymate" in life — someone with whom you can share, cry, laugh, and hurt. This is part of God's plan for marriage, family and the church.

A journeymate is someone *who cares for you.* You're not going to share your hurt with someone unless you're convinced that they care for you. You need someone who will stay close enough to know what you're going through and someone who will always be available to help. You must sense that they care for you just because of who you are, not because of what you do. It's good to know that in addition to God, there is another human (and sometimes, just one person is enough) who really cares for you.

A journeymate is someone *whom you can trust.* You'll also be reluctant to vulnerably share your hurt with someone unless you know you can trust them. A trustworthy journeymate must: be confidential about any sensitive information you may share, respond with compassion and acceptance to your hurts and pain, not use any information shared in confidence against you, and not allow any embarrassing information you share to adversely affect the relationship.

A journeymate is someone *who is available.* You may have a friend who cares about you and is trustworthy, but if they're not available when you need them, you'll still hurt alone. This is one of those times when availability is infinitely more important than ability. This highlights the need for Marriage Staff Meetings, periodic dates, and Family Nights.

Do you have a caring, trustworthy, and available journeymate? If not, developing such a friend should be an important priority in life. Your marriage partner can become your "best friend" and for single adults, friendships can be developed in the church to meet your needs for companionship.

Some people may have a sensitive journeymate, but they still hurt alone because they're unwilling to express their hurt. Our society, and often even the teaching of the church, presents a subtle message that, "It's a sign of weakness to grieve or mourn" or, "The more spiritual you become, you shouldn't feel hurt or loss, and if you do, you certainly shouldn't share it." And yet the Bible declares that:

"Blessed are those who mourn, for they shall be comforted" (Matthew 5:4).

"Blessed are the poor in spirit, for theirs is the kingdom of heaven" (Matthew 5:3).

"My (Jesus) power is made perfect in weakness" (II Corinthians 12:8).

And, as if we needed more evidence that mourning is alright, Jesus, the God/man often shared His hurts and disappointments:

"My soul is overwhelmed with sorrow to the point of death" (Mark 14:34).

"You will all fall away" (Mark 14:27).

"Jesus wept" (John 11:35).

If it was alright for Jesus to express hurt and mourn, it's certainly alright for us to.

A third reason why we often hurt alone is that our journeymate might not know how to properly respond to our mourning. When emotion is expressed (and mourning is an emotion), an emotional response must be given (Matthew 5:4). But quite often, we offer one of these four unproductive responses: logic or reasoning, criticism, complaining, or neglect. Here's how these might sound in a real life situation. Perhaps you've just lost a loved one in death and you're mourning your loss. A journeymate might tragically respond with:

Logic or Reasoning — "Don't cry, you know they're better off in heaven" or, "It's appointed unto man once to die."

Criticism — "Don't be so emotional, everyone goes through rough times."

Complaints — "Well, you know, I'm also hurt. He was my friend, too, and no one told me about his death until yesterday."

Neglect — "Don't focus on this one tragedy. Life's full of happy, positive events. Let's talk about some of those."

The only proper response to mourning is comfort.

Comfort includes understanding, empathy, gentleness, and affection. Here are some examples of what comfort might sound like:

"I can really see you're hurting."

"It saddens me that you are hurting."

"I'm committed to go through this with you."

"I'm sorry you hurt, I hurt for you."

"What can I do to help you?"

When we are hurt, if we share our hurt with a caring, trusting, available journeymate, and receive comfort, we will feel blessed (Matthew 5:4).

Do you ever hurt alone? Set aside time to be real and vulnerable with someone who cares.

Are you sensitive to others who may be suffering by themselves? Today, try to notice someone around you who would be blessed by your caring attention.

God never intended for us to be alone (Genesis 2:18); particularly when we're hurting. Begin taking time to purposefully reach out to your spouse, family, and friends to develop meaningful relationships which will be a source of refuge and comfort during the hurtful times of life.

Identity Crisis

For more than a decade, Jesse Ortiz didn't know who he was. A victim of amnesia, he wandered around the country working odd jobs and sleeping on the streets. He couldn't go home because he didn't know where home was. Somewhere along the way he picked up the name Danny Soto Castillo.

While on the streets of Tucson, Arizona, he received a vicious beating which turned out to be a blessing in disguise; evidently the blows to his head unlocked some biographical memory and a social worker put the information together and contacted his siblings in Fort Worth — who had been praying for his return for 12 years. They responded immediately and went to get their brother.

Jesse is now in good hands. He's home. He knows who he is and where he came from.

Christians often suffer from "selected amnesia." We forget who we are in Christ, where we came from, and where we're going in the future. Sometimes the negative statements that people have made about us hang on us like barnacles and we forget the positive declarations. We focus more on what the world and the devil say about us than what God has pronounced.

Listed below is the truth about who you are. This is a description of who God says you are. Recite these phrases out loud and apply them to your own life and then speak them to your spouse, children, and friends during special couple times, Family Nights or other gatherings.

- ◆ You're a person for God's own possession.
- ◆ You're a chosen person.
- ◆ You were fearfully and wonderfully made.
- ◆ He chose you before the foundation of the world.
- ◆ You are His workmanship, created in Christ Jesus for good works.
- ◆ You were created in the likeness and image of God.
- ◆ His Spirit lives in your heart, you can call Him Abba Father, Daddy God.
- ◆ You have been brought near to God by the blood of Christ.
- ◆ Because He loves you, He made Himself nothing, He took on the very nature of a bond servant, He humbled Himself and became

obedient unto death, even the death on the cross — that's how much He loves you.

◆ He reconciled you through the death of His Son, so that He can present you holy in His sight, without blemish and free from accusation.

◆ You are sealed in Him, with the Holy Spirit of promise.

◆ He has lavished the riches of His grace on you.

◆ You are forgiven.

◆ You are accepted.

◆ Therefore there is no condemnation toward you—you are free.

◆ He will never leave you or forsake you.

◆ He loves you.

◆ And so do I!

◆ Rejoice and be glad!

[Selected verses from: I Peter 2:9, Psalms 139:14, Ephesians 1:5 & 2:20, Genesis 1:27, Galatians 4:6, Ephesians 2:13, Philippians 2, Colossians 1:22, Ephesians 1:13 & 1:7, Colossians 3:13, Romans 15:7 & 8:1, Joshua 1:5 and Revelation 1:5.]

Priorities

His Colorado Buffaloes won the National Championship in 1991. They've been near the top every year since. He had 10 years remaining on a $350,000-per-year contract. Yet several days after Colorado thumped Notre Dame 41-24 in the Fiesta Bowl on January 2, 1995, Bill McCartney resigned as head-coach of the University of Colorado football team. His reason? "The glory of a man is his wife. Nothing tells you more about a man than what you see in his wife," McCartney said. "I began to see the neglect, pain, struggle, sacrifice, and denial in Lyndi's face." So at the age of 54, at the height of his career, McCartney stepped down. "Many of our best years are ahead of us," he said. "I want to do this while we both have a lot of energy and excitement about our lives."

Priorities. Everyone has them. Regardless of whether or not you've ever written yours down or even thought about them — you're "living out" what's important to you.

Most Christians, when asked to list their priorities, know some version of a "correct" answer: 1. God 2. Family 3. Ministry 4. Work. But while we may score well on this written exam, how are we doing on the "living" exam?

The following questions will help you assess the true status of your priorities. If you have to hedge on a lot of your answers or if you simply respond with a lot of "no's," you probably need to do some major restructuring in your life. It may not require the severe change that Bill McCartney made, but then again, it may. Continually ask yourself, "What's going to really matter 1,000 years from now?" and "What are the most important things in this life?" From God's eternal perspective, a very few things really matter: God, His Word, and people.

1. I spend regular, quality, uninterrupted time alone with my spouse at least once a week.

2. I spend regular, quality, uninterrupted time with my children at least once a week.

3. I know who my children's friends are, what they're doing in school, the stresses they're under, etc.

4. My spouse and children know me. I share with them my feelings and concerns.

5. I'm "approachable" by my spouse and family; they're not hesitant to vulnerably share their feelings or to approach me when I've offended them.

6. I keep up with family birthdays and other special occasions.

7. I spend regular, quality time deepening my intimate walk with God.

8. I am involved in a local church.

9. My friends at work and in the neighborhood know I'm a Christian.

10. If asked to quote a Bible verse, I feel comfortable sharing key scripture insights from memory.

11. I seek to share Christ with others in word and by example.

12. My family knows that I don't compromise moral standards by what I read and watch on TV.

13. My checkbook reflects my love for God and devotion to my family.

14. I often use my discretionary time to "enter into my family's world" and do what they want to do.

15. I attend church more than just on Sunday mornings.

16. I'm involved in some type of spiritual accountability group.

17. I have regular contact (visit, phone, or letter) with my extended family (in-laws, aunts, uncles, grandparents, etc.)

18. If asked to share a biblical perspective on my function in various relationships (as husband, wife, father, mother, sister, grandparent, etc.) I could do it.

Marriage Staff Meetings

Developing and maintaining marriage and family intimacy requires that husbands and wives spend quality, consistent time together. The external stresses of work, carpools, child raising, and checkbooks need not take their toll on marital "oneness" if couples will take the time to "manage" family events before they "manage" you! Even Jesus, during His public ministry, found it necessary to consistently withdraw from the crowds and spend time with His disciples for special times of sharing and encouragement.

It's inconceivable that a successful business could operate without regular staff meetings. Why then do most families try to operate without a regular time of planned communication? If it works in business, it will work for the family.

Here are some characteristics of a successful Marriage Staff Meeting.

◆ Schedule a time — don't leave it to chance!

Preferably, the staff meeting will be a "standing appointment," occurring the same time, same place each week. Perhaps a good time would be over lunch on Thursday, or Tuesday night after the children are asleep, or during Saturday morning breakfast. Some couples' schedule is such that the time has to change each week. If so, at least have a standard day and time that you schedule the staff meeting for the coming week, perhaps each Sunday evening.

◆ Prioritize the time — as much as possible, make it "inviolate."

Once the time is scheduled — protect it! Treat the appointment like it's the most important item on your schedule — because it is. Prioritizing the Marriage Staff Meeting will produce a renewed sense of closeness (one wife cried with joy when her husband remembered their staff meeting and turned down a golf date).

◆ Protect the time — from interruptions and distractions.

Find a "quiet" place at home, or if necessary, meet away from the home and office. Avoid phone calls or visitors if possible.

A fearful thought for many couples would be, "What in the world would we talk about?" A productive staff meeting might have this agenda:

◆ Consider Calendar Coordination — for the coming week.

What's planned? What's the children's schedule for the week? Who's working late? What social activities are scheduled (operate from a principle of agreeing on time commitments which affect the entire family before making these commitments)? Plan your next couple "date" and your next family outing. You'll even find that there's often great value in calendaring some of your lovemaking times!

◆ Listen to One Another — one spouse or the other may just need to talk.

When listening, establish eye contact and give undivided attention. Be quick to offer comfort, encouragement, and support. Avoid advice-giving, arguing, belittling, teaching, or lecturing. Be open to share hopes and dreams, feelings and insights about recent moodiness, and concerns and fears about the marriage, kids, money, and the future. The power of giving undivided attention allows you to enter into another person's "world" and really get to know them.

◆ Discuss Family Goals — and monitor their progress.

As marriage communication deepens, written annual goals need to be developed for the family and broken down into quarterly/monthly target dates. Goals and plans could be developed in these areas: marriage, social, financial, personal, family, educational, spiritual, and professional.

1. Does the budget look "tight" this coming week and if so, how can we all help?

2. What's our next planned major household expenditure and how could we all better "contribute" to bring it about?

3. Have we scheduled our family vacation? Reservations made? Itinerary set?

4. Have we decided on some new couple friends we want to get to know this year?

5. How are our personal goals progressing...reading, diet, exercise, hobby...and how can we encourage/support one another?

6. What aspects of church life do we want to be involved in this next quarter?

7. What's the next fun marriage "get-away" we have planned?

◆ Discuss Parenting Plans — if you don't become united on parenting issues, the kids will "divide and conquer!"

1. Discuss significant discipline issues; what seems to be working and what doesn't.

2. Plan family times together plus "quality times" with each child (a shopping trip for Mom and daughter, a golf date for Dad and son).

3. Discuss and agree upon parenting responsibilities and schedules for the next week. Who's needing help? Who's needing a "break" without the kids?

4. What goals seem reasonable for our children this quarter in the areas of behavior, attitude, and responsibilities, and how can we work together to achieve them?

◆ Engage in Productive "Criticism" — lovingly share areas of irritation, hurt, and disappointment.

In an intimate relationship, there will be the freedom to *"Speak the truth in love"* (Ephesians 4:15). A Marriage Staff Meeting provides a "neutral" setting in which "touchy issues" can be honestly shared in an atmosphere of acceptance and openness.

For instance you might need to share:

"I sure miss being alone with you, could we plan a 'date' together?"

"It would mean a lot to me if we could remain in agreement in front of the kids...and discuss any differences privately."

"Sometimes it seems your initial response to situations is negative. Could we talk about why that is and discuss how I could be helpful in encouraging optimism?"

"Last Tuesday I felt embarrassed when _____. Could we talk about it?"

◆ Share Words of Appreciation — for "who" your spouse is and "what" he/she has done.

Use your weekly staff meeting as a reminder that your spouse is a blessing to you! They do have good qualities!

For instance, you might share:

"Thanks for your help this week with the kids."

"I was reminded this week of how much I appreciate your diligence in seeing that things get done around the house."

"You are a very giving person, and it really showed this week when you..."

"I love you, just for who you are."

Establishing and maintaining a meaningful weekly Marriage Staff Meeting will be one of the most important steps you make in pursuing wholesome and intimate marriage and family relationships. Conflicts, hurts, and misunderstandings will be resolved, and a oneness will develop, allowing you to experience the joy of "walking together" according to Amos 3:3.

Maintaining Healthy Relationships...

Dealing with Conflict

Healthy relationships need constant attention. We often think that only bad relationships need attention but actually, the best relationships are those that are constantly worked on and "fine tuned." All types of relationships — husband/wife, friendships, employer/employee, parent/child — will benefit from the following scriptural principles that teach us how to keep relationships healthy and current.

"Do not let the sun go down while you are still angry" (Ephesians 4:26).

The first principle is: deal immediately with misunderstandings, hurts, and anything else that would cause you to be angry. This Scripture suggests that anger should not be internalized for more than twelve hours. Unresolved anger may lead to negative emotions such as bitterness, fear, guilt, condemnation and despair; and may eventually affect us in physiological ways such as insomnia, high blood pressure, anxiety, and headaches. Since there are no "perfect relationships," all relationships will inevitably produce hurts, and our reluctance to deal with them promptly causes us to internalize negative emotions that God never intended for us to bear.

"Speak the truth in love" (Ephesians 4:15).

The second principle is: deal with conflicts by sharing truth and always share the truth motivated by love.

First, this verse tells us *what* to speak — the truth. Whenever there's a conflict in interpersonal relationships, seek the truth. Many times we're upset over something we're misinformed about. Often, just talking out a situation — getting the facts — will dissolve many conflicts. Proverbs 18:17 says *"The first to present his case seems right, till another comes forward and questions him;"* which simply means — there's always two sides to every story.

But this verse also speaks to *how* the truth should be spoken, how it should delivered. Armed with the truth, you can't act like a "007 agent" with a license to kill, using the truth to maim and hurt; you must minister the truth in love. The Bible won't let you go up to someone in a crowd and blurt out "you're overweight," even though it may be the truth, because you'd be in violation of the "in love" clause.

If we ignore either admonition in this verse we'll become either a "hider" or a "hurler." "Hiders" don't share the truth; "Hurlers" share the truth— but not in love. Both approaches produce disastrous results. "Healers" but not in love. Both approaches produce disastrous results. "Healers" share the truth in love.

"A gentle answer turns away wrath, but a harsh word stirs up anger" (Proverbs 15:1).

The third principle is: learn to diffuse volatile conversations by speaking gentle words. What happens if you're verbally attacked by someone who hasn't memorized Ephesians 4:15? How do you respond to a "hurler?" The answer is not to hurl back, for then you fall into the trap of "returning insult for insult," a battle in which there is no winner.

What will neutralize anger? A gentle answer. What does a gentle answer sound like? Here are some examples: "I'm sorry this situation has disappointed you. Let's talk about it." "I want to do everything I can to restore peace to this relationship. Let's talk." "If I've done something to offend you, I want to know about it so I can make restitution."

Speaking a gentle answer doesn't mean you have to eat crow; it's not an open invitation for verbal abuse. Nor does it mean that someone can come "spill on you," then walk off, leaving you frustrated and confused. This verse is best applied to the first 90 seconds of a volatile conversation; it will diffuse an explosive situation before it gets out of hand. Once the conversation is manageable, then reconciliation is possible.

This week, see how often you can apply these three verses as you seek to maintain healthy relationships.

Developing Intimacy in the Family

"Enjoy your kids while you can, you won't always have them at home!"

Second only to your relationship with God, your family is your most important priority.

"Spend quality time with your family!"

We know we're supposed to. We know it would help. We know we'd enjoy it. Why *don't* we spend quality time with our family?

Perhaps it's because although we know what to do, we often don't know *how* to do it. Here are some practical suggestions on how to develop intimacy among family members.

Schedule Family Nights

Schedule an evening when all the family can be together and then protect the evening from conflicts and distractions. Start by having one a month, then bimonthly, then weekly. Don't turn on the TV, watch a movie, or anything else that would minimize conversation. Devote an entire evening (4-5 hours) to family activities such as:

Have dinner together.

Instead of eating out, cook at home. Take turns choosing the menu and cooking. Teach the children to cook; let everyone have their "specialty" dish they prepare. Occasionally, decorate for special occasions and highlight birthdays and holiday themes.

Talk together.

During dinner, involve everyone in both fun and vulnerable types of conversation. Begin by having everyone respond to "fun" questions such as, "What would you do if you inherited a million dollars?" or, "What would be your ideal vacation?" Then progress to more serious topics such as, "What would you like to be doing 5 years from now?" or, "When do you feel most loved?"

Communicate appreciation for one another. Put each person in the "spotlight" and ask each family member to share what they appreciate most about that person. Further affirm the person by showing loving affection — hug, kiss or embrace them while saying, "I love you."

Allow everyone to share how they're "feeling." Create a loving environment in which disappointments, hurts, fears, and other sensitive feelings can be shared. In responding to expressed feelings, avoid instructing, preaching, and criticism; instead, *"rejoice with those who rejoice"* and *"weep with those who weep."*

Play together.

After everyone helps with the dishes, engage in interactive games and activities such as board games, ping pong, charades, cards and sports activities.

Plan Family "Fun" Projects

Take turns letting each family member choose a "fun" project to do. Go horseback riding, fly kites, play tennis, camp out, search for a "special" antique, go fishing, plant a garden, visit a museum, or build something.

During the project, the focus should be on having fun together, not on "getting something done." If a project doesn't work out as planned, that's OK.

Try to keep a "souvenir" from your time together — a physical item that can serve as a future reminder of past good memories.

Intimacy is one of the joys of life. Be proactive in your pursuit of intimacy among family members!

Maintain Disciplines That Build Character and Deepen Spiritual Commitment

Journal of Gratefulness

On a regular basis, spend time adding to and reflecting on a family Journal of Gratefulness — a diary in which family members can record blessings, answers to prayer, or anything else for which they're grateful. This journal will help cultivate and maintain a spirit of gratefulness in the family and will serve to strengthen faith in God's future provision.

Scripture memory

As a family, memorize select Scripture verses, perhaps beginning with one per month. Periodically "check" each other on current and past verses. During Family Nights, discuss personal reflections on each verse.

Character studies

As a family, study key biblical characters and modern day men and women of God, looking for important character strengths and spiritual principles that guided their lives. Discuss how these principles could be applied to family member's lives.

Praying together

On a regular basis, share prayer requests and then pray together. A good time to do this is around the dinner table before the meal. Just expand the normal "prayer of thanks" into a 2-3 minute prayer time, allowing time for every person to pray. Be sure to also share answers to prayer.

Intimate relationships never just "happen," they must be cultivated and developed. And just reading this article won't help either.

> **Knowing what to do is not enough.**
>
> **Knowing how to do it is not enough.**
>
> **You have to do it!**

Here are some steps of action:

- ◆ Our next family night is scheduled for _____ (*date*).
- ◆ Our next Scripture verse to memorize is _____ (*verse*).
- ◆ We're going to begin a character study on _____ (*Bible character*).
- ◆ _____ (*family member*) is in charge of our next "family fun project" and it's scheduled for _____ (*date*).
- ◆ The menu for our next dinner together will be _____ (*menu*).

"Without a vision, people (and families) *perish"* (Proverbs 29:18).

Time Alone with God

"The first hour is the rudder of the day." Henry Ward Beecher

Spending time alone with God, on a daily basis, is one of life's "essentials." It's impossible to develop intimacy in any relationship without spending consistent time alone, and our relationship with God is no exception. Spending time alone with God has many advantages.

Our hearts find peace in His presence. Corrie ten Boom said, "Concentrate only on yourself and you'll be depressed; concentrate only on others and you'll be distressed; concentrate on Jesus and you'll be at rest." Isaiah put it this way, *"Thou wilt keep him in perfect peace, whose mind is stayed on Thee"* (Isaiah 26:3 KJV). In the midst of a chaotic, unpredictable world, we can find peace in His presence.

We receive instruction from life's "guidebook." A lot of Christians use their Bible like a drunk uses a lamp post — for support and not for illumination. But the Bible is the "Owner's Manual" of life. We can discover everything we need to know about interpersonal relationships, dealing with life's difficulties, and making decisions — if we'll search the Scriptures on a regular basis.

We receive personal guidance by spending time alone with God. George Washington Carver said, "At no other time have I so sharp an understanding of what God means to do with me as in those hours when other folks are still asleep. Then I hear God best and learn His plan!" The Psalmist declared, *"Your word is a lamp to my feet and a light for my path"* (Psalms 119:105). Neglecting the reading of God's Word is like stumbling through a dark house, refusing to turn on the lights.

We can share our thoughts and feelings with One who cares for us. It's OK to share with God exactly how you feel, it's even therapeutic. If you're happy, satisfied, peaceful — tell Him; but also share your feelings of anxiety, hurt, confusion, rejection, and weariness — those feelings that we're reluctant to confess, although they are common to human experience. Jesus never hesitated to tell His Father exactly how He felt, and He even did it in front of people! When anguishing on the cross, Jesus cried out, *"My God, My God, why have You forsaken Me"* (Matthew 27:46)?

Here are some practical suggestions on how to have a daily time alone with God.

Schedule the time; don't leave it to chance. Your time with God should be on your schedule, just like any other appointment. It's even advantageous to have a "standing" appointment — meet Him at the same time every day. Although it's not mandatory, many people find it best to spend time with God in the morning; if you wait until evening, you spend a lot of time giving a "damage report" and you'll miss the benefit of receiving fresh direction for the day. An early morning devotion seemed to be the habit of both the Psalmist and Jesus: *"In the morning I will order my prayer to Thee and eagerly watch"* (Psalm 5:3), *"Very early in the morning, while it was still dark, Jesus got up, left the house and went off to a solitary place, where He prayed"* (Mark 1:35).

Meet in a secluded, quiet place. Most people have a "special place," a specific location where they meet the Lord. It may be a specific room, a comfortable chair, looking out a particular window, or on a patio. Wherever the location, it should be quiet and protected from interruptions.

Follow a plan. If you don't have a set agenda, you'll probably lapse into day-dreaming and the time will be ineffective. Adopt a set pattern and follow it every day. A simple but effective plan would be to divide the time into three equal parts: praise, Bible reading, and prayer. During the praise time express gratitude to God for who He is and what He has done. The praise time can be enhanced by playing a praise tape. When reading the Bible, it's helpful to use a systematic reading schedule. This is one of the particular benefits of the *Intimate Moments Devotional Guide* as each day's Scripture reading focuses on a specific intimacy need which God has met in our life and then how we might be a good steward of God's grace as we give to others. 52 intimacy needs are addressed—one each week. Another approach might be to spend an entire year studying the wisdom of Proverbs. Read the book once each month, starting with chapter one on the first day of the month, then chapter two on the second day and so on. During the prayer time, spend time talking with God but also take time to listen; prayer is a dialogue.

Enjoy your time with God. If your quiet time ever becomes burdensome, something's wrong. Don't ever meet with God because you think you "have to," and don't feel guilty if you miss a few days. We're dealing with a love relationship, not a contractual obligation.

Just as God provided "daily bread" for the Israelites' physical needs, He wants to provide nourishment for our emotional and spiritual needs. Besides that, He loves us and delights to spend time with us. Amy Carmichael wrote of the blessedness of spending time with God:

> *"Walking the dawn-wind, Jesus, heavenly Lover,*
> *In the still beauty of the waking morn,*
> *Unveil Thyself to me, and with the vision*
> *Shall come the strength for trials yet unborn."*

When Obedience Is Not Enough

Ten men — their flesh rotting, extremities gone. Outcasts of society, they were forced to identify their own contagious condition by crying, "Unclean, unclean." Isolated from loved ones, they were united by a common plague — leprosy. Word had spread, even to the leper colony, about a young Jewish man named Jesus, who, with tenderness and compassion was healing those who would call upon His name. So in their desperation they cried out. But instead of crying, "Unclean, unclean," they cried, "Jesus, Master, have mercy on us!"

And He did.

His instructions: "Go show yourself to the priest." And as they went they were healed. They obeyed — not only the direct command of Jesus but also the laws of purification as stated in the Mosaic law.

As their skin became pure, multiple emotions flooded their hearts: bewilderment, ecstasy, hope. But in one man's heart the overwhelming sentiment was — gratefulness.

He reversed his direction, ran back to Jesus, fell at His feet, and with a loud voice praised and thanked the one who had made him whole. The priests were always on call at the Synagogue and there would be ample time — later — to be declared pure. But at this particular moment his heart was fixed on one thing — saying thanks, expressing gratitude, to Jesus.

Did Jesus reprimand him for not completing His instructions? No, He received the man's praise and even voiced disappointment that the other nine did not follow suit. [Adapted from Luke 17.]

Obedience is often not enough.

Unfortunately, many people's concept of living the Christian life consists only of rigidly and legalistically obeying a set of guidelines and principles. To them, the integrity of their relationship with Christ is determined by how well they know and obey the rules. Technically, their approach is adequate; relationally, their approach is wanting.

True gratitude is never demanded. Hoped for? Yes. Appropriate? Always. But never demanded.

Take a moment to check some of your spiritual vital signs:

◆ Do you live in obedience to God's word? If not, obedience is the first priority.

◆ Do you have an "attitude of gratitude?" If not, consider all that He has done for you and respond appropriately. Give Him thanks.

It's interesting to note that gratitude brings its own reward. The leper that returned to give praise to Jesus received a threefold reward: fellowship with Christ — the man had a personal encounter with the Lord; spiritual insight — he learned that it was his faith in Jesus that had healed him, not his "going and showing himself to the priest," as the others had thought; and, he received a new direction life — Jesus told him to "go your way," obviously never to be the same again.

An attitude of gratitude will also impact your outlook on life. Henry Ward Beecher once said, "If one would give me a dish of sand and tell me there were particles of iron in it, I might look for them with my eyes and search for them with my clumsy fingers and be unable to detect them; but let me take a magnet and sweep through it and now would it draw to itself the almost invisible particles by the mere power of attraction. The unthankful heart, like my finger in the sand, discovers no mercies; but let the thankful heart sweep through the day and as the magnet finds the iron, so it will find, in every hour, some heavenly blessings. Only the iron in God's sand is gold!"

All relationships will benefit from words of gratitude. How long has it been since you expressed gratitude to your spouse? Your friends? Your children? Your Lord?

Well, that's too long!

"And be thankful" (Colossians 3:15).

Grace – The Enablement for Intimacy

Intimacy is often defined as, "genuinely knowing another person, and becoming caringly involved in their life as we allow them to know us in a similar way." Additionally, we can identify various "intimacy needs" such as acceptance, attention, affection, appreciation, and comfort. Still there's a "power" outside ourselves that must enable the real experiencing of intimacy. The complexity and overwhelming "neediness" of our human condition means that relationships tend to move toward deterioration.

It's what happens when two humanly "bankrupt" partners join forces together in marriage. Larry Crabb observes that each partner becomes like a "tick" on a dog — "I'm here to take from you." — only to find in such a marriage that we have two ticks and no dog!

Our only hope is outside ourselves and this "closed system" of humanism. An unlimited source of love, acceptance, comfort, and forgiveness is needed to enable and sustain an intimate relationship. Such a source is available, and His name is Jesus. The Bible calls His divine contribution . . . grace!

Grace Initiates

"For by grace you are saved" (Ephesians 2:8-9).

Divine grace initiates our intimate relationship with God. It was Christ who humbled Himself, took on the form of a servant and became obedient to the point of death (Philippians 2:7-10) . . . that we might become a partaker of the divine nature (II Peter 1:4). Noted Bible scholar Donald Barnhouse speaks of our undeserved gift of grace in this way "love that goes upward is worship; love that goes outward is affection; love that stoops is grace." Christ "stooped" from heaven, entered into my world and gave Himself! What an example! Having partaken of this divine initiative, one spouse initiates caring involvement in a partner's life and it's this initiative that genuinely communicates, "I was thinking of you," and "I care." In a similar way, parents can take the initiative to really know their children and enter into their world as good stewards of this divine grace.

Grace Liberates

"It was for freedom that Christ set us free" (Galatians 5:1).

It's also grace that frees us from the penalty of sin and grants eternal life so that one day we will be free from the *presence* of sin (Titus 3:5). But "much more" than this, it's grace that can liberate us from the *power* of sin in this life.

◆ There's liberty from selfishness . . . freeing me to see and give to the needs of others.

◆ There's liberty from criticism . . . freeing me from judging others.

Just as Christ looked beyond my faults and saw my needs, I'm now free to look beyond others' faults and see their needs. Instead of judging another's behavior, we have the freedom to give unselfishly in meeting their intimacy needs (Philippians 2:3).

Grace Motivates

"As good stewards of the manifold grace of God" (I Peter 4:10).

Living in the awe and wonder of all that we *have* and *are* in Christ — motivates a stewardship of grace.

This life of intimacy with God and others is not lived out in obligation or duty. There wells up within the believer such a joyful gratefulness and humble appreciation that giving unconditionally to a spouse, child, friend or even our enemy is uncontrollable! Out of our innermost being will flow rivers of living water that nourish intimacy in human relationships (John 7:38). Grace is infectious, contagious . . . the love of Christ is now *"constraining"* us (II Corinthians 5:14).

Grace Lubricates

"be filled with the Spirit . . . always giving thanks . . . being subject to one another" (Ephesians 5:18-21).

Chuck Swindoll in his excellent writing *The Grace Awakening* speaks of the marriage "oiled by grace." It's grace that lubricates the inevitable "rough edges" of our humanness. The demands and "closeness" of marriage and family inevitably bring the human rough spots to the surface . . . but the "intimate" relationship ministers the oil of God's grace:

- ◆ As acceptance is granted . . . in spite of "performance" (Romans 15:7).
- ◆ As edifying words are shared to build -up and encourage (Ephesians 4:29).
- ◆ As personal responsibility is emphasized in focusing on our walk with our Savior (Romans 14:10-12).

As we experience God's grace in relationships — we come to enjoy more of an "abundance," the kind that's exceeding, beyond what we could ask or think (John 10:10, Ephesians 3:20).

Prioritize the Marriage . . . Then the Family!

There are Few Broken Eggs in a Whole Nest

Maid, taxi driver, tutor, nurse or whatever it takes, Janet is determined to be all that her kids need. She genuinely loves her two children and she's very devoted to them. Most of her time, energy, and emotions are focused on the well-being of her kids.

Paul is the most hard-working dedicated father you could find. During the week, he's committed to making a good living for his kids. He also goes to the soccer games and attends the recitals on the weekend.

She's a great mother and he's a good father, but in their zeal to be "super mom and super dad," they're neglecting one another and their relationship is beginning to suffer. They're aware of the problem but rationalize their neglect by thinking, "My partner's an adult, he/she can take care of herself/himself; the children need me—if I have to choose between the two, my spouse can wait." They don't realize that the quickest way to damage the kids is to weaken the marriage relationship. Conversely, one of the best ways they can love their kids is to love each other.

It is vitally important that children see mom and dad "prioritize" the marriage relationship as the first of God's ordained human relationships. Children feel secure as they see a strong level of intimacy between their parents. An intimate foundation in marriage also allows children the freedom to grow up. To have a healthy marriage and family, both the parents and children must sense that mom and dad love each other and are committed to one another.

This principle is a critical factor in "blended families." There's often an internal pressure for parents to attempt to "make up for" a broken home by prioritizing the children above the new marriage. Just the opposite is what is needed! A key "loss" children have experienced from a broken home is the loss of a role model in seeing an adult man and an adult woman live out Christlike, committed love toward one another. This is exactly the gift a new marriage can give to children in the blended family!

Here are some practical suggestions on how the uniqueness and integrity of the parents' relationship with each other can be developed, protected and "prioritized."

1. Reserve some *knowledge* that will be *private* among parents, such as: marriage goals, personal goals, educational plans, and ministry ideas.

2. Reserve some *feelings* that will be *private* among parents, such as: unresolved negative feelings toward certain family members, co-workers, and others.

3. Reserve some *topics* that will be *private* among parents, such as: sexual intimacy specifics, unhealed personal family history, financial business, and family status.

4. Reserve some *times* to be *private* among parents, such as: weekly staff meetings, sexual intimacy times, date nights. Get a lock on your bedroom door. Children should knock before entering.

5. Verbally acknowledge the *oneness* of your relationship in front of others. You can: greet your spouse first when entering the house, use pet names for each other (honey, sweetie), and avoid calling each other "Mom" and "Dad."

6. *Physically acknowledge the "oneness" of your relationship in front of others.* You can: greet each other with a hug, allow the children to "catch" you hugging, physically stand or sit with each other during family outings and social gatherings, hold hands, sit together while watching TV.

7. Allow children to see signs of *caring* such as the giving of small gifts, flowers, opening doors, serving each other, or doing chores for each other.

8. Go out on *dates* alone at least twice a month. This is a time for the children to see you dress up and model for them proper dating habits and good manners.

9. During times that family *gifts* are bought (Valentine's Day, Christmas), buy a unique and special gift for your spouse. Avoid giving the same type of gift that you give to your children. (If you give your children a card for Valentine's Day, send your spouse flowers or perfume.)

10. *Support* your spouse when he/she *disciplines* the children. You can confer together in private if you do not agree.

11. *Support* your spouse's *parenting policies* when they are absent:
    ◆ Support the rules that have already been set, if rules should be changed, both parents should discuss the changes together and privately.
    ◆ If a child asks you for something, see to it that the child has not already asked the other parent first.

11. *Support* your spouse's *parenting policies* when they are absent:

12. Show *praise* and *appreciation* for your spouse in front of the children; avoid asking for agreement from the children.

13. *Encourage* your spouse in front of the children. These are observations that consider character qualities of your spouse, apart from what they *do*.

14. In front of the children, make *positive* comments concerning the physical attractiveness of your spouse. Statements like, "I love that dress on you, Honey." "You have such beautiful brown eyes."

During your next Marriage Staff Meeting, discuss these fourteen items. Ask your spouse to honestly share with you, ways in which you have not prioritized your marriage relationship, and specifically, ways in which you have chosen the children over your spouse.

Ask forgiveness for times when the relationship was hurt because of your neglect or wrong priority. You might even need to talk to the children, explaining to them how you have been wrong and how you intend to correct the situation.

The well-being of your marriage and your relationship with your children will be strengthened as you prioritize the intimacy of marriage.

Hiding, Hurling, Healing

According to psychologist Charles Speilberger of the University of South Florida, Tampa, males and females are about equally likely to experience anger in everyday life but the two sexes often handle anger and aggression in strikingly different ways. Females often "explain away" shabby treatment from others by trying to understand the cause of the behavior. Men don't make so many excuses for other people...they feel more like expressing their anger — and they do. For instance, relative to how women deal with anger:

◆ *Only 9% of women say they typically deal with anger by directly confronting the person with whom they are upset.*

◆ *35% wouldn't express anger even to a family member, 9% wouldn't to a friend.*

The result of hiding anger? According to psychologist Zahn-Waxler, adult women feel more guilty and anxious about aggression, and they worry about hurting people more than men do. Perhaps that's why women's depression rates soar far above men's, partly because they're trained to stuff their anger. Depressed women often have great difficulty expressing anger.

At the other end of the spectrum, many men are "macho boys" who punch at every offense. (Adopted from an article entitled *The Traits of Wrath in Men and Women*, by Marilyn Elias, *USA Today*, August 11, 1994.)

Pain is inevitable. We live in a world of hurts, disappointments, and misunderstanding, so it's not a matter of *if* we'll become angry, the issue is, when we become angry, *how are we going to deal with it?* What is the proper way to deal with anger?

First, let's discuss the wrong way to deal with anger. As mentioned in the above article, most people either suppress their anger and become "hiders," or they lose control and become "hurlers." (Remember Adam and Eve's responses after the Genesis 3 "Fall" . . . they first "hid" from God, and then when confronted, "hurled" or blamed others.) Both approaches produce painful outcomes.

Hiding

Hiding pain hurts you and others. It may seem like the easy way out is to ignore pain and to "stuff it"; but to disregard the truth of your hurt sets in motion a damaging cycle that affects both you and your relationship with others.

"Hiding" hurt can feed anger and bitterness. You may find yourself pretending on the outside and seething on the inside.

"Hiding" hurt can prompt subsequent retaliation and rebellion. You may find yourself like the little school boy sent to the corner for misbehaving—he was sitting down on the outside but standing up on the inside! This "standing up" on the inside can later be expressed by being uncooperative, selfish, insensitive, or can even produce more overt actions. Periodic explosions would not be uncommon. An attitude of "I'll show you," might lead to retaliation by escaping into work, substance abuse or an affair.

"Hiding" hurt can undermine your sense of worth and prompt feelings of condemnation. Ignoring hurt can eventually damage our sense of identity and worth. We might begin to think, "I'm not worth being treated any better than this" or, "There's something wrong with me or I'd have more love and less hurt." Furthermore, significant and long-lasting damage can occur if we think our needs, hurts and pain seem too unimportant to mention.

"Hiding" hurt can contribute to harmful relational and physical side effects. Internalized or suppressed emotions like anger, bitterness, guilt and anxiety are often associated with physical complaints such as ulcers, high blood pressure and skin rashes. "Anger turned inward" is a common expression for certain forms of depression. Inhibited sexual desire, particularly in women, is frequently associated with unresolved emotional/stress issues.

"Hiding" hurt hinders others from knowing the "real" me! To hide my true feelings is to pretend and wear a "mask" of protection. Intimacy is hindered and relationships remain shallow. It's often difficult for loved ones around me to sense that I can genuinely feel love for them if they don't see and hear that I can feel pain.

Hurling

"Hurling" to attack hurts you and others. Hurlers often want to get even, "You hurt me — I'm going to hurt you." They may attack with hurtful words, temper tantrums, shouting matches or physical abuse. The result is always damaging.

"Hurling" adds feelings of guilt. Considerable research has shown that simply "venting" anger and hurt doesn't release it; most of the time, the anger remains and then we feel guilty because of how we may have attacked or hurt another person. Psychological and physical consequences are often associated with unresolved guilt.

"Hurling" often undermines our sense of worth. After a hurling attack, we may internalize thoughts such as, "I can't believe I stooped so low with my words" or, "I'm no better at self-control than a non-Christian." This sense of self-blame, and shameful condemnation will steal our sense of joy and peace.

"Hurling" focuses on a problem (or person) you can't fix! One of the most frustrating things about attacking others is that it rarely does any good and usually makes matters worse. A key reason for this is that your attacking focuses on someone you can't change! The focus is shifted away from the only person you really can be responsible for—you!

"Hurling" undermines the foundation of close relationships. One of the worst things about hurtful words and actions is that they can't be "taken back." Trust is undermined as past events are used to hurt others. The emotional pain inflicted by harsh words, even if they were not really meant, will linger in the heart of a wounded spouse or friend long after the attack is over. Often, only the bad times are remembered and hope gives way to despair and the joy of closeness is lost. "Hiding" feelings of anger doesn't work, "hurling" doesn't work either. The only viable solution is to "heal" the anger by applying biblical principles.

Healing

First, when you get angry, *"Share the truth in love"* (Ephesians 4:15). If someone offends you — tell them; but be sure to tell them in a loving way. "Hiders" don't speak, "hurlers" speak but not in love.

For example, rather than saying, "I'm sick of the way you talk to me when you're really angry at your boss" share, "I can see that you're upset and yet when you take it out on me, it really hurts."

Second, forgive your offender (Ephesians 4:32). Forgiveness is primarily a choice. Choose to forgive even if your offender doesn't ask your forgiveness and even if his behavior doesn't change. Forgiveness will help you *"get rid of all bitterness, rage and anger"* (Ephesians 4:31), as you recall the gratefulness you feel for Christ having forgiven you. Perhaps it is in the act of forgiving our offenders that we most accurately reflect the attitude and actions of Christ. In becoming more like Him, we will experience His peace, joy and rest.

Sharing the Bible with Your Family

"And these words, which I am commanding you today, shall be on your heart; and you shall teach them diligently to your sons and you shall talk to them when you sit in your house...when you walk...when you lie down...and when you rise up" (Deuteronomy 6:6-7).

Under-girding our families with the foundations of biblical truth is obviously important, but how is it to be done? Try announcing to your children, "Let's get our Bibles and study some rules or 'Thou shalt nots!' " and see what kind of response you get.

What's the key to meaningful family devotions? What should family devotions include? God gave Moses and the children of Israel important insight into propagating the word of God from one generation to the next. Deuteronomy 6 describes an "as you go through life" approach to sharing the word of God.

This approach includes both a structured time of sharing and a sensitivity to "teachable moments," times in our lives when life's events present a prime environment for instruction. For instance, a teachable moment may be when a child is rejected by a friend and it seems fitting to speak of a sympathetic Jesus who also was despised and rejected. A teachable moment may occur when the family pet dies and we can share about a Christ who wept over Jerusalem and at the tomb of Lazarus. Perhaps when the family faces financial stress we can remember that Christ promised the birds of the air that He would provide for them, and how He arrays the flowers of the field and that in like manner He will provide for those who seek first His kingdom.

But in either "teachable moments" or more structured devotional times during Family Nights, what should be the main "curriculum?" Should we emphasize key historical events in Scriptures, significant parables, or various instructional teachings? While each of these at times will need to be emphasized, the Psalmist gives us key insights in "how" to teach the word:

"The law of the Lord is perfect, restoring the soul" (Psalm 19:7a).

God's laws of "principles" are what restore us from the inside out, principles such as God's sovereignty, avoiding evil, and learning to make wise decisions. Parents should focus attention on building these foundational principles into family life. But again, "how" do we best share such principles with our children? The Psalmist also shares:

"The testimony of the Lord is sure, making wise the simple" (Psalm 19:7b).

The Hebrew word translated "simple" is often used to describe those who are "child-like," those not yet mature in their understanding (see also

Proverbs 1:4). What is it that brings wisdom to the simple? It's the testimonies of the Lord as He works in the life of His people. This is why the Bible is filled with examples from the lives of patriarchs, prophets, psalmists, kings, disciples, and others. Therefore, in family devotions it's very profitable to focus on character studies from the lives of Bible characters. As these "testimonies" illustrate God's laws and principles they bring wisdom to the immature. In I Corinthians 10:11 we are told why these testimonies were recorded, *"These things happened as our example and they were written for our instruction."*

For instance, a study of the life and testimony of Joseph would illustrate God's principle or law of sovereignty as time after time God brings forth provision and deliverance, climaxing in the powerful scene of Joseph before his brothers saying, *"You meant it for evil but God meant it for good"* (Genesis 50:20). Tamar's failure to live out God's principle of avoiding evil (II Samuel 13) could make a powerful, positive impact on an adolescent's concept of maintaining moral purity. A study of Lot's selfish decision, based on temporal gain with moral risk (Genesis 13) could highlight important principles of wise decision making.

These Bible testimonies provide the opportunity for family members to vulnerably share similar challenges, and to share examples from their own life journey.

When families encounter God's principles and see them "lived out" through Bible testimonies, they will reap the promised blessing of restoration and wisdom (Psalm 19:7). It's no wonder that the psalmist declared God's word as, *"more precious than gold"* (Psalm 19:10).

Learning to Identify People's Needs
by Listening to What They Say

We all have important intimacy needs. These needs are "built into the DNA of the human race," and they serve as catalyst for our motivation and they strongly affect our behavior. Many people are unaware of these needs in their lives and therefore don't know how to correctly express their needs when they are neglected. Even if we acknowledge our "neediness," we often forget to properly express our needs to our loved ones.

Listed below are some phrases you might hear from your spouse, children, or friends. Beside each phrase, write down the need that's being expressed by each statement. Possible needs are: acceptance, approval, security, respect, encouragement, attention, support, comfort, affection, and appreciation.

1. "You're too busy." _____
2. "Look what I did." _____
3. "Do you mind asking my opinion?" _____
4. "Will you always love me?" _____
5. "I just can't do this." _____
6. "I feel out of place." _____
7. "I've had a bad day." _____
8. "I feel like a failure." _____
9. "Could we spend more time together?" _____
10. "I'm really upset!" _____
11. "Hold me." _____
12. "Would you help me?" _____
13. "I have a big nose." _____
14. "What do you think of what I've done?" _____
15. "I can't do anything right!" _____
16. "I've had it!" _____
17. "You're always making all the decisions." _____
18. "I just want a place we can call home." _____

[Try using this exercise to prompt discussion of individual intimacy needs during a Marriage Staff Meeting or during a Family Night. This exercise is from the Intimate Life Ministries' booklet entitled Top Ten Intimacy Needs.]

The Four Stages of Marriage

Marriage is a journey. It is a dynamic, ever-changing experience. Just as an infant develops from a passive and fragile newborn into an overactive two-year-old into a peer conscious teenager — in like manner, marriages and families "develop" through predictable and recognizable stages. Awareness of these stages and the challenges they present can serve as important "warning signs" for what lies ahead, allowing time for caution and preparation.

Listed below are four common stages of marriage and some of the challenges that each stage presents and suggestions for action and discussion.

Stage 1 – New Love

The honeymoon begins and two individuals start blending their lives. This is a picture of married couples without children. Average time of this stage – 2 years.

Developmental Challenges and Practical Suggestions

Freedom from Power Struggles

- Power struggles are inevitable when needs for attention and affection aren't met. Increase "dating" times and show plenty of affection.

- Commit to make significant decisions only in oneness; if you don't agree, wait and pray until oneness comes.

- Set aside time for weekly staff meetings to discuss decisions; avoid acting independently.

- Learn to look underneath power struggles to identify your partner's true intimacy needs, then give to meet them.

Freedom to establish individual identity

- Take turns choosing fun activities to do as a couple. The blessing is in being together, not the activity.

- Begin speaking of "our" home, children and finances—not "my" and "mine."

- Together, read good books on developing oneness in marriage.

- Do a topical Bible study using a concordance to identify all the "husband" or "wife" passages.

Freedom from expectations

- Begin a journal of gratefulness, focusing on your partner's strengths and your gratefulness.

◆ Be prepared to "give up" expected roles you thought your spouse would assume based upon what you saw modeled in your home growing up.

◆ Develop close Christ-centered couple friends and notice that there's no such thing as a perfect mate.

◆ Strengthen your devotional life with a prayer journal, and begin to redirect your expectations to God and allow Him to prompt your giving.

Freedom to confess and forgive

◆ Establish a goal of *"not letting the sun go down on your anger"* (Ephesians 4:26).

◆ Don't rationalize your wrongs but admit them; this is a crucial sign of maturity.

◆ Be specific about your wrong, "I was selfish. I hurt you with my anger."

◆ Saying "I was wrong" is better than saying "I'm sorry." Then ask for forgiveness.

Freedom from in-law control

◆ Begin at least one family tradition which doesn't involve either family-of-origin.

◆ Make plans for a family vacation, your holiday activities, and holiday traditions.

◆ Be aware of unresolved emotions which were carried over from the family-of-origin and properly deal with them.

◆ Begin "sharing the truth in love" with parents concerning your desires, plans, and hopes.

Freedom to enjoy sexual oneness

◆ As you "part" in the morning and "re-unite" in the evening, affectionately embrace.

◆ Read together and discuss the book *Solomon on Sex* by Dillo.

◆ During times of sexual intimacy, take turns focusing entirely on giving to your spouse as you learn what is particularly meaningful to him/her.

Stage 2 – Shared Love

The first child arrives and love must now be shared. This stage involves families with children through age 12. Average time of this stage – 12 years.

Developmental Challenges and Practical Suggestions

Freedom from wrong priorities

- ◆ Occasionally ask your spouse to write down for you: "What do you see as my top five priorities?" The answer will probably be very insightful.

- ◆ Schedule weekly staff meetings to maintain open communication.

- ◆ Annually, review all family and individual commitments to purge "stale" obligations.

- ◆ Keep inevitable hurts healed by confession and forgiveness so "avoidance" patterns don't develop.

Freedom to accept imperfections

- ◆ Maintain prayerful awareness of God's work in your life, including needed changes.

- ◆ List your spouse's "imperfections" and note how each one could merely be a strength that needs some tempering or refinement.

- ◆ Complete a Bible word study on the word "accept" and memorize key scriptures dealing with accepting one another.

- ◆ Spend time recording blessings you've received from your spouse, this will help prompt gratefulness and acceptance.

Freedom from hidden agendas

- ◆ Read and discuss good books on family issues.

- ◆ Review material on intimacy needs and identify what your spouse might have missed — this often helps define how you can best love him/her.

- ◆ Look at the things you seem almost "driven" to give your children (attention, affection, etc.). These are needs you may have missed as a child.

- ◆ Learn to look "underneath" your marital conflicts for unhealed "growing-up" pain.

Freedom to "give" and not take

- ◆ Make careful observation of your response to disappointments and irritations in dealing with your partner — if you stop "giving," your giving is conditional.

- Review your devotional life for additional opportunities to develop gratefulness for God's blessings.

- Complete a Bible word study on the word "love" (agape) which is God's giving love.

- Become a "student" of your spouse to more accurately understand his/her most important intimacy needs.

Freedom from doubting God's provision

- Don't "panic" when you see your partner's weak points; keep hurts healed and prioritize giving.

- Focus often on your partner's strengths of character, gifts, and talents and express appreciation for them.

- Take thoughts "captive" and cast them down when your mind begins to wander (II Corinthians 10:3-5).

- Memorize and then meditate on passages which speak of victory over fear (II Timothy 1:7; I John 4:18-19).

Freedom to "balance" one another

- Do not make any major decisions about plans, money, kids, etc. until there is a oneness of mind with your partner.

- Admit often to your partner how incomplete your ideas and perspectives are and appreciate the balance of his/her input.

- Practice deferring to your partner's leadership in areas where he/she is obviously more gifted or insightful.

- As you pray together, acknowledge God's plan of two people becoming one, and how He can accomplish that even though partners are different.

Stage 3 – Mature Love

The first child becomes a teenager and love had better be mature! Families remain in this stage until the last child leaves home. Average time of this stage – 15 years.

Developmental Challenges

Freedom from adolescent control

- Always keep in mind that neither of you see any issue totally objectively; we all have blind spots and bias; you need one another, so stay together.

◆ Remember that this period is a balance between freedom and responsibility. Trust your teen in new areas and as they act responsibly, trust them with more freedom.

◆ Don't be pressured into giving immediate answers to teen requests; encourage them to plan ahead on their requests, giving Mom and Dad time to talk about them privately.

◆ Give "warnings" in firm loving ways, "Yes you can use the car *after* you're finished helping your mom."

Freedom to prioritize "us"

◆ "Date" your spouse! Plan it, talk about it, look forward to it and watch your teens learn from it.

◆ "Escape" with your spouse, preferably each quarter for a night to refocus, relax, and rekindle.

◆ When you go out alone, trust your kids to the care of relatives, friends, or older siblings; sooner or later they need to learn responsible behavior.

◆ Now is a good time to explore new hobbies and common interests which can be enjoyed together as the "nest" begins to empty.

Freedom from losing personal identity

◆ Make time just for you – time to relax, have fun, and be personally enriched. You won't have anything left to give unless you "replenish" yourself.

◆ Start new hobbies or common interests, dream new dreams, develop new goals.

◆ Seize the rare "alone" moments with your partner just to be quiet, to hold one another, and to communicate his/her specialness.

◆ At least annually, "purge" your "to do lists" and standing commitments, gaining freedom to "be," not just "do."

Freedom to enjoy kids

◆ Make family nights a priority, even if the kids groan and complain. Keep family nights fun and let the kids have input regarding what you do. Be sure to communicate that the most important aspect of these times together is, "I just enjoy being with you."

◆ Occasionally laugh with your teens over some of your own teenage failures, rebellion, and pranks; let them know you're a real person.

◆ Hug and verbalize love even if it's not reciprocated or acknowledged; teens need it even though they think it's not "cool" to admit it.

- Look for a particular strength in each child, showing interest, appreciation, and encouragement.

Freedom from unhealed childhood pain

- Look "underneath" your hurts and fears to see if your personal unresolved pain is contributing to the struggle you're having with your teenagers. It's often difficult to give to your teenager's emotional needs like comfort, reassurance, praise and freedom if you did not receive them when you were a child.

- Discuss with your spouse how your concept of parenting may have been both positively and negatively affected by how you were raised.

- Give your spouse freedom to express childhood sadness and losses. Don't criticize in-laws for their failures, but empathize with your spouse.

Freedom to deal with inevitable loss

- Difficult times can bring a couple closer together. Be there for one another during times of pain and loss.

- Grieve losses together, giving comfort and support. Don't pretend you don't hurt and don't intellectualize or give advice, rather weep with those who weep.

- The inevitability of losses underscores the importance of building a strong marriage through the early stages of marriage. If this foundation is not built, inevitable loss can pull couples apart.

Stage 4 – Renewed Love

The last child is "launched" from the nest and love can now be renewed. This stage lasts an average of 28 years.

Developmental Challenges

Freedom to enjoy life as it is

- In this world we have tribulation! But contentment with God and His provision of Himself and meaningful others will free us to live abundantly "in the present."

- Focus more on what you *have* rather than what you *don't have*; reflect often on your blessings and develop a grateful spirit.

- Accept limitations of energy, mobility, and resources as you enjoy one day at a time, treasuring life's special moments.

Freedom from fearing the empty nest

◆ Times of marital re-kindling should be frequent as the two become one again. Frequent dates, sharing common interests, and sexual initiatives will reassure both partners of good times ahead.

◆ Fears of children leaving home with unresolved pain can be removed through vulnerable times of sharing regrets, and confession and forgiveness.

◆ Re-prioritizing the marriage relationship above career, hobbies, children or friends provides security.

Freedom to build new dreams

◆ Opportunities of ministry and impacting the lives of others should be explored, discussed, and planned for.

◆ Encourage your partner to dream new dreams, "What are some things you have always wanted to do? I want to be supportive of you as you seek to fulfill them."

◆ Assess your strengths, interests, and untapped potentials. As you consider the future, think about the "life message" God has given you.

Freedom from fearing intimacy

◆ Vulnerability and openness are very important in dealing with anxieties, feelings of inadequacy and hopes for the future.

◆ Renewing romance through surprises and frequent get-away weekends helps reassure your partner about the future.

◆ Keeping hurts healed through confession and forgiveness plus sharing needs in loving vulnerability will protect the relationship from bitterness and fear.

Freedom to be "friends" with kids and grand-kids

◆ Advice, control, and discipline of children has been replaced by seeking their counsel and rejoicing in their strengths and accomplishments.

◆ Vulnerable times of sharing with your adult children can help heal any old hurts and sharing reflections and insights from your life journey promotes understanding and friendship.

◆ Resist criticism of your children's parenting; instead, view unmet needs in the life of grandchildren as opportunities to minister attention, affection, and approval, as needed.

The concept of family life cycles provides more than a descriptive identification of families at different periods of married life. It is a frame of reference that allows us to identify key stages that greatly affect individual behavior and interaction within the family. For example, as the cycle shifts from newly married to the child-rearing stage, couples are required to modify their roles. Whereas once they were only husband and wife, now they're both mates and parents. As their lives undergo significant changes, they must face different demands, learn new skills and develop new attitudes.

Family life-cycle stages help explain the constantly changing demands and expectations of family interaction. Being aware of these stages helps us to be prepared for the inevitable challenges and stresses accompanying them.

Set aside time with your spouse to discuss these stages and the practical suggestions in order to develop some goals for the new year. Discussing these stages and challenges during family nights with school age children and adolescents should produce a lively discussion, deepen understanding, and help equip children and teenagers for their own family life experiences.

The Surpassing Value of Knowing Christ

I count all things to be loss in view of the surpassing value of knowing Christ Jesus my Lord" (Philippians 3:8).

Priorities — life seems so complex. The competing demands of employment, family responsibilities, social involvement and Christian responsibility endlessly cry out for our time and attention. Misplaced priorities are wrecking marriages, families, churches, ministries, and society.

There are late nights of work, committee meetings, social activities, church activities, children's sports, school activities, tutoring, studies, chores, etc. Older children, particularly teenagers, succumb to the pressure of over-involvement, seeking to "belong" in some important group. Parents, often feeling a sense of false-guilt, let their children "do more" than they got to do as children. Feeling the pressure not to "miss out," families are being torn apart by the tyranny of busyness. Today's families are very busy, but very "barren" — barren of intimacy, focused often on "making a living" but unsure as to how to "impart one's life" (II Thessalonians 2:8-9).

Amidst this complex set of competing priorities, it seems fitting to reflect on the Apostle Paul's exhortation to the Corinthians, *"I am afraid lest your minds be led astray from the simplicity and purity of devotion to Christ"* (II Corinthians 11:3, NAS).

Apparently there's a certain "simplicity" in our devotion to Christ that clarifies and empowers all other priorities. The apostle's maturing walk with the Savior seems to have led him to this simple secret: *"That I may know Him, and the power of His resurrection and the fellowship of His sufferings"* (Philippians 3:10, NAS).

That I might know Him
— identifies who He is

Paul's passion to intimately know this One who has so loved Him far exceeds any other priority! It's here that intimacy and "right priorities" begin. The challenges of each day and the demands of every relationship must not be met by "mere humans" but by ambassadors for Christ (II Corinthians 5:20). Practically, this life of intimately knowing my Lord includes:

- ◆ **"Hearing" Christ** during quiet, reflective times allows me to "be still and know that **He is God.**" *"This is my beloved Son in whom I am well pleased, hear Him"* (Matthew 17:5).

- ◆ Time **"with" Christ** is important . . . in praise of **His working** and in worship of **His character.** *"And He appointed twelve, that they might be with Him"* (Mark 3:14).

- **Alone with Christ** in prayer and meditation becomes important to me, particularly as I see **His dependence** upon the Father. *"And in the early morning, while it was still dark, He arose and went out and departed to a lonely place and was praying there"* (Mark 1:35).

- **Seeing Christ** in His "humanness" with compassion and tears gives insight into how He will live through me. *"And when He approached, He saw the city and wept over it"* (Luke 19:37-41).

. . . the power of His Resurrection
— identifies me with Christ

This truth makes available to the believer – "resurrected life" – a source of love and empowerment of the Spirit that is constrained to selflessly give, care, and love. It's this life that ministers to our intimacy need for acceptance, affection, forgiveness, and security. Having received such abundance, we are then challenged to be a *"good steward of the manifold (many-faceted) grace of God"* (II Peter 4:10).

- Because He died and rose . . . **I can live in Him**, drawing on His strength, wisdom and love. *"It is no longer I that liveth but Christ who lives in me"* (Galatians 2:20).

- Because He died and rose . . . **I can live as Him**, extending His presence into my world by the power of His spirit. *"As Christ is . . . so also are we in this world"* (I John 4:17).

- Because He died and rose . . . **I can live for Him**, as I live as His ambassador, sharing His life and love. *"He died for all, that they which live should not henceforth live unto themselves, but unto Him who died for them and rose again"* (II Corinthians 5:15).

- Because He died and rose . . . **I can live to Glorify Him**, responding in gratefulness and "wonder" at the grace given me. *"For you have been bought with a price; therefore glorify God in your body"* (II Corinthians 6:20).

Finally, the Apostle declares this aspect of "surpassing value:"

. . . the fellowship of His Sufferings
— identifies Christ with me

Christ was indeed who He claimed to be — the last Adam, the God-man, the Word having become flesh. He was, at the same time, all God and fully human. In his humanity, He has identified with me. Having been tempted in all ways, acquainted with sorrow, despised and rejected, He can understand me. In exploring the depths of His humanity, I find the reassurance that I'm not alone . . . and receive the hope to carry on.

◆ Christ understands our struggles, trials and pain . . . therefore we're not without support. *"For we do not have a high priest who cannot sympathize with our weaknesses"* (Hebrews 4:15).

◆ Christ ministers as One who has received compassion . . . therefore we're not without comfort. *"He was despised and forsaken of men, a man of sorrows and acquainted with grief"* (Isaiah 53:3).

◆ Christ identifies with our loneliness and distress . . . therefore we're not alone. *"My soul is deeply grieved to the point of death"* (Matthew 26:38).

◆ Christ comprehends our pain, that rises from a grieved heart . . . therefore we're not judged or condemned. *"He looked around at them with anger, being grieved at the hardness of heart"* (Mark 3:5).

Intimacy in marriage, family, and the church begins with this surpassing value of knowing Christ.

The Ministry of Support Groups
Called to be Burden Bearers

It is unthinkable that this could have happened to the Apostle Paul — but it did:

"At my first defense, no one came to my support, but everyone deserted me. May it not be held against them" (II Timothy 4:16).

During his time of greatest need, the esteemed apostle and leader of the first century church — was deserted.

When Paul wrote these words, which were the closing comments in what would become his final letter, he was a prisoner in Rome. He had just had a preliminary hearing before the Emperor; an important "first defense" because if the arguments were properly presented and the magistrates thoroughly convinced that Paul was not a troublemaker after all, he could have been set free. But instead, he was sentenced to die and would soon be executed.

The sobering aspect of this incident is the fact that there was a Christian church in Rome — a large church whose *"faith was proclaimed throughout the whole world"* (Romans 1:8).

We all know that people are fickle, but this seems to be rather extreme. Where were all the Christian brothers and sisters? Why didn't they show up? Why didn't they testify on behalf of their elder statesman? It's not that they didn't know about Paul's need, or that they just forgot — they *deserted* him.

The serious nature of their neglect is grievously declared by Paul when he says, *"May it not be held against them."*

It is sin to abandon a brother in need. It's not just something we should feel sorry about, it's something we must confess.

In Ephesians 6:2 we're commanded to *"Carry each other's burdens, and in this way you will fulfill the law of Christ."* Corrie ten Boom reminds us that, "God doesn't make any suggestions," and this sounds like a command.

Succinctly stated, we have a biblical mandate to comfort those who need comforting, to stand with friends in times of distress, and to carry one another's burdens. This is a major part of following Christ and a prerequisite for experiencing the abundant Christian life.

Do you know someone who is hurting? To be more specific, do you know anyone who is unemployed, separated from his/her spouse, has a wayward child, is suffering physically, is facing a lawsuit, is lonely?

In one church there are several ladies who meet every Monday night for the expressed purpose of encouraging one another. They all share one thing in common; their husbands have left them and they realize they just can't make it on their own without some help. A group of men in their late forties/early fifties meet once a week, just to help each other through the crisis of mid-life. Men and women who were raised by an alcoholic parent have received great freedom by meeting with one another to share the fears and hurts that inevitably come from abusive parents.

Counselors call these "support groups" but perhaps we could call them "burden bearers groups." Regardless of what you call them, they're needed and they work. One reason support groups work is because people who are suffering or have suffered in a particular area are more capable of under-standing and giving comfort to others who are suffering in like manner. In 430 B.C. the historian Thucydides said it this way: "It was in those who had recovered from the plague that the sick and the dying found most compassion." In the first century A.D. Paul said it this way:

"The God of all comfort, who comforts us in all our troubles, so that we can comfort those in any trouble with the comfort we ourselves have received from God" (II Corinthians 1:4).

Andrew Davison tells of a life-changing lesson he learned from the great humanitarian, theologian, and physician, Albert Schweitzer. "Dr. Schweitzer was eighty-five years old when I visited his jungle hospital at Lambarene, on the banks of the Ogowe River. One morning, the equatorial sun was beating down mercilessly, and we were walking up a hill with Dr. Schweitzer. Suddenly he left us and strode across the slope of the hill to a place where an African woman was struggling upward with a huge armload of wood for the cookfires. I watched with both admiration and concern as the eighty-five year-old man took the entire load of wood and carried it on up the hill for the relieved woman. When we all reached the top of the hill, one of the members of our group asked Dr. Schweitzer why he did things like that, implying that in that heat and at his age he should not. Albert Schweitzer, looking right at all of us and pointing to the woman, said simply, 'No one should ever have to carry a burden like that alone.'"

Lord, make us burden bearers.

CHAPTER SEVEN
Intimacy Research Findings

Intimacy Research Findings

Summary: Divorce is only slightly less common among church families.

Findings: Divorce rates after 5 years of marriage

◆ 53% when couples had **no** practicing religious faith

◆ 42% among Catholic couples

◆ 41% among Protestant couples

◆ 30% among Jewish couples

Source: "Religions Homogamy and Marital Duration Among Those Who File for Divorce in California," Jerry S. Moneker and Robert P. Ranken; Journal of Divorce and Remarriage 19 [1993]: 223-246.

Summary: "Living Together" before marriage brings many DANGERS

Findings: 18 Month Study of Cohabiting Couples

◆ Only 30% actually married although many more had "planned to"

◆ More likely to divorce if they later marry . . . divorce rate is 75%

◆ More permissive sexual attitudes after marriage . . . "less restrictive" on later adultery

◆ Males **less likely** to be employed full time and more likely to assume "lower occupational status"

◆ Females **more likely** to be employed full time than "married" wives

◆ Poorer current relationships with parents, families and in-laws

◆ Poor previous relationship with parents . . . particularly father . . . feeling "distant" from dad during childhood

Source: "Cohabitation and Marriage: Retrospective and Predictive Comparisons," John D. Cunningham and John K. Antill; Journal of Social and Personal Relationships 11 [1994]: 77-93.

Summary: The inter-generational pain of divorce is significant

Findings: Selected Studies on Long-term Effects of Divorce

- ◆ Children rejected/ridiculed at school are more likely to come from broken homes

- ◆ Broken homes seem to have offered little example and exposure to **positive** strategies for initiative and maintaining friendships or resolving conflict constructively

- ◆ Such children . . . are at risk for "long-term maladjustment"

- ◆ Boys involved in **violent** misbehavior were 11 times more likely to live in homes without their father

- ◆ Promiscuity among young girls is "significantly" higher from single parent homes

- ◆ Alcohol abuse among teens from broken homes is notably higher . . . "A collapse of family structure causing traumatic separation experiences"

- ◆ Children from broken homes are "significantly less likely to graduate from high school"

Source: "The Relation Between Fifth and Sixth Graders Peer-Related Classroom Social Status and The Perceptions of Family and Neighborhood Factors," Bartholemy & Lawrence A. Kurdek; Journal of Applied Developmental Psychology 14 [1993]: 547-556.

"Risk Factors for Violent Behavior in Elementary School Boys;" Jonathan L. Sheline, American Journal of Public Health 84, [1994]: 661-663.

"Predictors of High-Risk Behavior in Unmarried American Women;" Stuart N. Seidman, Journal of Adolescent Health, 15 [1994]: 126-132.

"Teenage Alcohol Drinking and Non-Standard Family Background;" Matti Isohani, Social Science & Medicine 38 [1994]: 1565-1574.

"Simplicity and Complexity in the Effects of Parental Structure on High School Graduation," Roger A. Wojtkiewicz; Demography 30 [1993]: 701-715.

Summary: Teenagers from broken homes are six times more likely to become involved in delinquent behavior

Findings: Juvenile Delinquency Study

- 13% came from homes in which both the biological mother and father were present

- 33% came from homes in which parents were divorced or separated

- 44% came from homes where parents had never married . . . typically only one parent present

Source: "Family Status of Delinquents in Juvenile Correctional Facilities . . ." Wisconsin Department of Health and Social Services, April 1994.

Findings: Study of Conduct Disorders in Children

- Exposure to parental divorce is strongly associated with higher rates of conduct disorder (behavior problems) in children—six (6) times more likely

Source: "Family Risk Factors, Parental Depression and Psychopathology in Off-Spring," Michael Fendrich, Virginia Warner and Myrna M. Weissman; Developmental Psychology 26 [1990]: 40-50.

Summary: Higher suicide rates from broken homes

Findings: Teenage/young adult suicide study

    ◆ Suicide rate among adolescents and young adults has increased 500% from 1946-1985

    ◆ Strong predictor of suicide is the "family structure index" — a composite index based on the annual rate of children experiencing divorce and children presently in single parent families

Source: "Trends in White Male Adolescent, Young Adult Suicide: Are There Common Underlying Structural Factors," Patricia L. McCall & Kenneth C. Land; Social Science Research 23 [1994]: 57-81.

Findings: Teenage/young adult suicide study

    ◆ Suicide rate are four (4) times higher among divorced males (age 25-54) and three (3) times among divorced females (ages 20-39) when compared with married males and females in the same age brackets

Source: "An epidemiological Investigation of Potential Risk Factors for Suicide Attempts," K.R. Petronis et al.; Social Psychiatry and Psychiatric Epidemiology 25 [1990].

    ◆ Suicide attempts were eleven (11) times greater for the separated and divorced, as compared with other marital groups

Source: "New Micro-Level Data on the Impact of Divorce on Suicide, 1959-1980: A Test of Two Theories," Steven Stack; Journal of Marriage and Family 52 [1990]: 119-127.

Summary: Spouse abuse related to intimacy breakdown

Findings: State-by-state comparison of spouse abuse statistics

- ◆ Economic inequalities and other "social" inequalities were **not** found to increase risk of violence
- ◆ Strong correlationship between "spouse assault" and "social disorganization index" which includes:
  - — divorce rates
  - — single parent households
  - — number of households reporting **no** religious affiliation
- ◆ Findings are consistent with social disorganization theory which holds that crime and other deviant behavior are more likely to occur in a society in which the disruption of traditional social patterns weakens the attachment (intimacy) of individuals to mutual moral commitments and standards

Source: "State-to-state Differences in Social Inequality and Social Bonds Relation to Assaults on Wives in U.S.," Murray A. Straus; Journal of Comparative Studies [1994]: 17-24.

Summary: School drop-out rates effected by marriage and family breakdown

Findings: School drop-out study

- ◆ Single parent household is a **key** predictor of "who will drop out of school"
- ◆ Two-parent families are a key dimension of neighborhood social structure without which communities lose the ability to monitor teenage behavior

Source: "Do Neighborhoods Influence Child & Adolescent Development," Jeanne Brooks-Gunn, et al.; American Journal of Sociology 99 [1993]: 353-95.

- ◆ Children from single-parent households are nearly three (3) times more likely to **drop out of school** when compared with students from intact families (7% drop out from intact families: 20% from single parent families)

Source: "Race and Ethnicity, Family Structure and High School Graduation," Gary D. Sandifur, Sara McLanahan, Roger A. Wojtkiewicz; Institute for Research on Poverty Discussion – Paper No. 893-89 [Aug 1989].

Summary: Parents need to reclaim their parenting role

Findings: Study of Parenting "Insecurities"

- ◆ Homicide is leading cause of death for males 18-25 years old
- ◆ Parents seem to have lost their "executive function" in the home through:
  - — single parenthood
  - — both parents working
  - — threats of divorce
  - — breakdown of extended families
  - — home distractions through TV/video/computers
  - — over-extended parent and child schedules
- ◆ Parents are very uncertain as to how to discipline their children
  - — often trying to "delegate" discipline to the schools/ church
  - — parents bombarded with advice from media, educators, physicians, etc. to the point they do not "trust" their own judgment
  - — parents insecure and afraid to parent their children

Source: "Have Parents Lost Control of Their Children," Gunnar B. Stickler & Margery Satter; Clinical Pediatrics, April 1994, 249-251.

Summary: Characteristics of Strong Families

Findings: Study of stable, long-term "happy" marriages (30+ years)

- ◆ Commitment to keep family "top priority" — when outside pressures (work, finances, social engagements, etc.) threaten to remove family from its top priority, members of strong families take action and make sacrifices if necessary to preserve family well-being

- ◆ Shared time together as a family unit is high in both quality and quantity

- ◆ A religious or spiritual orientation to family life provides a foundation of values, hope and security

Source: "Research on Families," Maria Krysan, Kristin A. Moore & Nicholas Zill, U.S. Dept. of Health and Human Services, May 10, 1990.

CHAPTER EIGHT

Intimate Life Resources

Intimate Life Resources

Intimate Life Newsletter – A monthly publication with helpful, practical articles and information on how to maintain healthy relationships.

The Pursuit of Intimacy – A book based on the *Pursuit of Intimacy* seminar taught across America; particularly intended for use in Marriage Intimacy classes.

Intimate Moments – A daily devotional guide to help couples establish an intimate relationship with God and each other. The authors share their personal struggles and victories as they voice their prayers to God.

Intimate Encounters Workbook – A practical workbook on developing intimacy skills in marriage and other relationships; particularly designed for use with couples, groups, mentoring and counseling.

Intimate Encounters Audio Tape Set – A series of teaching tapes that coincide with the Intimate Encounters Workbook. Couples may want to listen to these tapes as they complete the workbook exercises. Ministers or lay leaders may want to use these tapes to supplement their preparation for teaching the Intimate Encounters material.

Intimate Encounters Video Tape Set – A series of teaching tapes that coincide with the Intimate Encounters Workbook. Couples may want to view these tapes as they complete the workbook exercises. Ministers or lay leaders may want to use these tapes to supplement their preparation for teaching the Intimate Encounters materials in large group settings.

Intimate Life Experiential Teaching/Class Curriculum – Includes weekly outlines, lesson plans, questions and reproducible masters which corresponds to the sixteen chapters of the Intimate Encounters workbook.

Parenting with Intimacy – This book explains how to incorporate Intimate Life principles within a family. Parents are given insightful, practical information on how to create an intimate relationship with each child. The material is applicable through the different life stages: for parents of newborns to parents with adult children. The unique needs of single parenting and blended families are also addressed within each chapter.

Intimate Family Moments – An interactive tool for family devotions. Biblical principles are taught through activities that a family does together. The twelve lessons include a Bible Drama, ideas for Intimacy Disclosures and a selection of activities that teach the lesson objective. Activities are suggested for all ages: preschool, grade school, middle school and high school. Designed for individual families, Sunday School curriculum, home school, as well as retreat settings.

Parenting with Intimacy Workbook – A practical workbook on developing intimate relationships within the family. A challenging look at how to truly "know" your children, let them "know" you and then how to become lovingly involved in their lives. Designed for couples and parenting groups.

Parenting with Intimacy Audio Tape Set – Tapes of the *Parenting with Intimacy* seminar. These tapes may be used in conjunction with the *Parenting with Intimacy Workbook* or *Intimate Family Moments*.

Intimate Life Study Guides – Short (50-80 page) studies dealing with marriage and family interpersonal relationship skills and other intimacy topics. Recently published - *Top 10 Intimacy Needs.*

Top 10 Intimacy Needs Video Tape Set – A series of video tapes produced by the Intimate Life Team that takes the viewer on a step-by-step journey through the materials in the *Top 10 Intimacy Needs* book. This video series is suitable for individual, home or church group use.

Intimate Life Radio Production Sets – Audio sets of popular topics which aired on the daily *Intimate Life Radio Program.* Topics have recently included: *Sex and Intimacy, Straight Thinking, Aloneness, Giving Worth to Kids, Leaving and Cleaving, The Intimate Life Message* and *Emotional Responding.*

Intimate Life Radio Specials – One hour audio tapes designed to explore, in depth, the applications of intimacy principles and issues such as the *Healing Power of Intimacy* and *An Intimate Encounter.*

Intimate Life Video Series – Intimate Life Professional Associates and popular speakers such as Josh McDowell, Max Lucado and Dennis Rainey speak on a variety of intimacy topics and issues. The video tape sets available are: *Intimacy with God, Parenting with Intimacy* and *Intimate Relationships.* Individual video cassettes are also available.

God's Plan for Intimacy Sermon Series – Sermon resources including outlines, illustrations, word studies and supporting research plus teaching, preaching and promotional audio tapes. Also included as suggested follow-up resources for the congregation are the *Intimate Moments* devotional, *Top 10 Intimacy Needs* booklet and Special Newsletter #1.

Intimate Life Ministry Orientation Kit – A package of materials which includes the *Pursuit of Intimacy* book, *Intimate Moments* devotional, *Intimate Encounters* workbook, *Time of Refreshing* music audio cassette, *Intimate Encounters* Audio Tape Set and a one year subscription to the *Intimate Life Newsletter.* This package is particularly focused on providing the key resources for beginning a marriage and family ministry.

Intimate Life Handbook – This handbook describes the many parts of the Intimate Life Ministries, including our purpose, our message, information on the development of an Intimate Life Ministry in the local church and leadership training, supporting material on the Intimate Life Message and other resources.

Songs of Intimacy – Music collection of cassettes, CD's, split tracks and songbook of songs which will encourage hearts toward God.